THE DEVIL'S GAMBIT

PRAISE FOR *THE DEVIL'S GAMBIT*

"A thought-provoking book, challenging us to seriously examine building our treasure in heaven versus our treasure on earth."

Dr. Andrew Essig,
Professor of Political Science,
DeSales University

"Most of us invest without ever even questioning its morality. Marc Lozano takes a closer look at the reasons why we invest, what investing means, as well as the societal consequences, and then he examines the whole system in light of biblical ethical principles. Essentially, is it ok to make money without labor? This book is a must read for anyone who claims to be a Christian and is interested in financial matters."

Matt D'Antuono,
author of *Philosophy Fridays* and
A Fool's Errand: A Brief, Informal Introduction to Philosophy for Young Catholics

"I pride myself on being good with money, personally and professionally. Frankly, when Marc first introduced me to the ideas in this book, because I enjoy being open-minded and economics generally, I wrestled mightily with them. It was like tasting my tongue or seeing my eyes—and it was actually fun! His premises are presented simply and are truly groundbreaking. Deep down, going back decades to my youth, I have always sensed that something was rotten with the system. Like I was the sucker in the room, financially and morally. You will probably sense something similar, so seek the truth. Fear nothing. Here be monsters. Slay them."

Bud Macfarlane,
Bestselling novelist and Founder & CEO
of The Mary Foundation

"Marc stepped into deep waters, perfectly challenging the stock market and where we reap but do not sow. At the very least this book will alter your view of reward for no labor and charge every Christ-minded reader to challenge the norm and to think from a kingdom perspective about reaping what we sow!"

Danny Crenshaw,
Founder of Kingdom Coffee Houses

"Whether or not you agree with everything in *The Devil's Gambit*—which dives right into topics on which most of us have strong opinions—this book is well worth the read for anyone committed to living in the world but not of the world."

Philip Cerroni,
Associate Ethicist at National Catholic Bioethics Center

THE DEVIL'S GAMBIT

HOW THE STOCK MARKET DESTROYS WEALTH AND VIRTUE

MARC LOZANO

CHRIST CENTERED CAPITAL

Published by POPbooks
February 2025

Print ISBN: 978-1-7327582-8-5
Ebook ISBN: 978-1-7327582-9-2

Cover design and interior layout by Faith & Family Publications
Editing by Lorraine Ranalli, lorraineranalli.com

Address inquiries in writing to:
support@christcenteredcapital.com

Printed in the United States of America

TABLE OF CONTENTS

INTRODUCTION

What is the common good?

What is the stock market and how does it work?

What is true labor?

How ought we approach new and challenging ideas?

These questions and more will be answered before I tackle the seemingly odd combination of finance, philosophy, and Christian social teaching.

Global finance, the international banking system, and the way in which governments treat and use currency are problems in the world but these topics will not be addressed directly in this work. Instead, we will explore the secondary exchange market, commonly referred to as the stock market, and the evils it inflicts upon society. Although this subject could be covered extensively, I present here a brief and direct case study with practicable solutions.

Two complementary theories form the foundation of my crusade against the stock market. The common good must not be sacrificed and we ought not divorce compensation from labor.

In his encyclical Mater et Magistra (On Christianity and Social Progress), Pope John XXIII defines the common good as "the sum total of social conditions which allow people, either as groups or as individuals, to reach their fulfillment more fully and more easily." I will reference this phrase often in my arguments against the stock market, objections to my arguments, and my responses to those objections. The common good, simply stated, is a society that fosters as many saints as possible for the glory of God through just means. (Think: good families and communities raising saints rather than an oppressive authority creating martyrs through persecution.)

Compensation, therefore, should be earned only through labor that produces a good or service that promotes the common good. This keeps the pursuit of wealth married to the dignifying nature of labor. When the acquisition of wealth is divorced from truly productive labor, our base desires of the flesh inevitably take over and vices run rampant. When vices run rampant, the community and the family suffer.

I firmly believe the stock market runs counter to the common good and is void of true labor, thus the compensation received from stock market investing is ill gotten. Such profits manifest in detrimental and prevalent evils in society without most investors or participants realizing it.

The evils about which I speak include greed, sloth throughout society, nuclear family decay, predatory inflation, economic "growth" utterly detached from the shrinking goods and services the common man receives (I call this Abstract Dominant Economics), and an ever-expanding dehumanizing globalized financial system. These societal ills, coupled with teachings from scripture and the Church Magisterium, should compel us to oppose the stock market.

Although counterintuitive, given our deeply ingrained culture, my claim is that the security exchanges themselves are intrinsically evil. Stock exchanges have a net negative impact on society and have severely hindered the common good. Typical objections to my bold assertion point to the many jobs, innovations, financial independence, and economic growth resulting from stock exchanges. I will address each of these concerns and more throughout this book.

My purpose is not to urge you to change your financial practices, but to present a path to freedom from economic slavery and a more rightly ordered society which produces saints.

DEALING WITH DIFFICULT IDEAS

I did not set out to be controversial, but the radical nature of my thesis renders it so because it creates mental, emotional, and even physical discomfort. If you accept the ideas presented here, then prepare to undergo changes in how you view and approach wealth and investing. These changes are radical because they go against the entire financial culture that surrounds us.

As the Bible tells us more than 100 times, "do not be afraid." If what I propose does not ring true for you, then you will have no reason to change your current habits. If, however, my proposition strikes a nerve, then you and your loved ones will enjoy a more peaceful, happier, and contented life when you seek to align your approach to finances with Christian teaching. My goal is to educate as many people as possible about the evils of modern investing and prompt action that will combat those evils. When we Christians are made aware of the destructive effects that the stock market wreaks on individuals, families, and local communities, its immorality becomes painfully evident. The inspiration to take action follows.

THE ROLE OF VIRTUE

When dealing with difficult ideas, it is imperative that we invoke the virtues of charity, gentleness, and patience, and pray for an open mind and open heart. No matter where you line up on this issue, charity is crucial because finances can be an emotional hot button for many people. Finances are, and always have been, tough to talk about. Hence, the old cliché of not talking about politics, religion, or money.

Make no mistake, I wrote this book to communicate the idea that the stock market is immoral and to challenge you to re-evaluate how you invest. However, very little to no effective communication can take place if my ideas are thrust upon others in an arrogant and derogatory manner. I aim to be charitable in my approach and ask you to do the same, should you be inspired to share this information.

Historically, few have been convinced of something because they were called an idiot or a depraved sinner. (I happen to be one of these people who needed to be called an idiot, but the thickness of my head could only be cracked by a battering ram, which is not the case for the majority.) I've concluded, therefore, that being gentle is best when trying to convince others that something is immoral. Being gentle does not mean being wishy-washy about convictions. It means we should be capable of listening with compassion and making points charitably.

One of the main reasons I aim to be gentle and charitable when making my case about the stock market and similar types of investing is because of how deeply stock market investing is rooted in our culture. Sometimes a thing can be immoral but not sinful due to our ignorance and personal situation. Think of the child stealing a loaf of bread to feed his younger siblings. Is stealing bread immoral? Yes, but is the child guilty of sin? Perhaps not depending on his knowledge and circumstance.

For generations we in the first world, and especially Americans, have been taught that getting a nice 401(k) plan and buying high-quality stocks and ETFs (exchange traded funds) are actions a financially responsible person should take. There is, of course, substance to this line of thought. Investing for the future is not immoral in and of itself and acting in a financially responsible way is a Christian and a natural virtue. The stock market is perceived as an easy and accessible way for people to build future wealth, which is why we have adopted it so eagerly over the last few generations. Naturally, therefore, when attacking the stock market, there is going to be a lot of resistance. Nothing less should be expected.

After all, the ideas of this book, in a way, are attacking how the bank accounts of most are structured. If my theories are accepted, it may become even more difficult than it already is for some to provide for their families. In short, the deep cultural roots of stock market investing can make conversations about the morality of investing problematic.

Also, the relative newness and subtlety of the stock market are both reasons why patience and gentleness are needed when expressing its evils. The market may have deep cultural roots, but they were established over a relatively short period. The stock market has only been mainstreamed for a few generations, leading to some ignorance and indifference among the public, a status quo that financial institutions would like to maintain.

This ignorance and indifference are only amplified by the fact that stock market investing does not appear as heinous or egregious as extortion, bribery, money laundering, and fraud, which society recognizes as sinful. Needless to say, these factors create an arduous uphill climb for the person who wants to communicate the message that "playing the market" is opposed to Christian virtue. Patience, charity, and gentleness will be our friends in conversations about the morality of investing.

CONTEMPLATION

Following is a list of questions with which I wrestled when I was initially challenged about the stock market—the source of my financial success and provisions on which my family relied. I invite you to reflect on these questions, one at a time. Wrestle with them, make notes. Ask additional questions. Most importantly, pray about them as you continue reading.

- On its face, does the act of buying at a low price with the intent of selling at a higher price, without personally adding value to the good or service the company produces, seem like something a Christian should do?
- Is any value added by the investor, who does not in any way produce the good or service being sold by the company?
- Because owning a stock traditionally merits the right to vote at shareholder meetings, does this warrant being compensated for these votes? In what other context is being "paid" to vote moral? For instance, wouldn't being paid to vote in a political election be utterly repulsive, vile, and corrupt?
- Which is more important: pursuit of sanctity, eternal salvation, and service to loved ones or securing a "comfortable" retirement oriented almost entirely toward personal indulgence and not working?
- How often do you turn to our Heavenly Father for guidance about what to do with your material wealth?
- Do your stock market investments and retirement accounts build up the Kingdom of God, or do they fund its destruction?
- Have you ever complained to others or resented Big Tech's and other industries' patently negative cultural influence and oligarchical practice in collusion with governmental authorities, while relying on these same corporations as the foundation for growing your personal wealth?

- Consider the western world's generations-long trends of having fewer or no children, relying on abortion as last-ditch contraception, slavishly climbing the career ladder, having family members living thousands of miles apart, and replacing community services traditionally provided by local churches with impersonal nationalized welfare programs. Are these positive or negative developments of the past few generations?
- If negative, why have these trends become culturally dominant? Could our prevailing investment practices contribute to these social pathologies? If so, what is your responsibility?
- Given that we are always dependent on someone or something, are you actually more comfortable depending on "the market" or upon your own extended family and community?
- Do you care more about being a saint or about being a millionaire? Is it possible to be both? Does one make the other more difficult? What does scripture mean by "the love of money is the root of all evil" (1 Tm 6:10)?
- What do you love?

PART I

BACKGROUND

CHAPTER 1

THE PERSONAL JOURNEY THAT GOT US HERE

I studied economics and finance in college, earning a bachelor's degree and an MBA, but it was during my years as an undergrad that I got a taste of Wall Street. I learned quickly that I did not care for the hustle and bustle, or the 70-hour work week associated with "The Street."

I also disliked my first role after college. I was a financial analyst for a hospital; it was boring. In an effort to follow my dream of working in the NBA, I applied to an entry-level communications job. Basketball was a long-standing passion for my wife and me. We met while playing for the same college.

To my surprise, I landed an interview with the NBA. It did not take me long to realize that my summer job as a basketball skills trainer for IMG Academy, an elite boarding school and professional athlete training facility in Florida, is what piqued the interest of my hiring manager, not because the experience was relevant but because she was obsessed with football. IMG is known for sports, especially football, and she was the head of a booster club for a high school football team in New Jersey. She wanted to pick my brain about IMG because her team was traveling there to play in the coming months.

At the end of our meeting (it was hardly a job interview), she acknowledged the disconnect between my resume and the job for which I was applying but still offered me a position monitoring games to collect video clips. Although entry-level, this was a demanding job in terms of time and pressure. I had to clip video of every game and with help from co-workers deliver the clips to TV outlets around the country almost in real-time. If I missed a remarkable play, I would meet the wrath of any number of "bosses." I had a proclivity for this work because I tend to be obsessive about details, and I know the game of basketball well. My attention to details was noticed.

After a year, I was invited to work for the business operations department, where I would remain for the following five years. I moved between titles within the department but was essentially a budget creator and manager of people. I was a business operations manager for LP&E (Live Production and Entertainment), which was one of many revenue generators for the NBA. LP&E was responsible for global events that came with multimillion-dollar budgets. I managed the budgets, the staff, the vendors, and the contractors, ensuring the events were executed successfully.

I then transitioned to the content operations department, which was responsible for curating all the entertainment the NBA produced. It's important to note that the NBA is an entertainment company and not necessarily a sports company. The team I worked on managed various departments within the NBA conglomeration and around the globe. Ours was a team of about a dozen people who were responsible for over $100 million worth of budgets.

Prior to the pandemic, I traveled a lot, attending each all-star game and the Junior NBA Global Championships. I enjoyed the latter most because they were wholesome. The best of the best youth from around the world competed in these championships, and all related events focused on the kids and their families. While the Junior NBA Global Championship helped the NBA identify talent from around the world, it was a loss leader for the organization and a public display of charity.

During my six years with the NBA, I slowly realized my dream job was a living nightmare.

I had graduated college as a Christian in mind but not in spirit. I gained the intellectual part of Christianity while trying to disprove my then-girlfriend's firm Catholic beliefs. I was a good student. I enjoyed learning. I even completed both my undergraduate and graduate degrees in just four-and-a-half years because of the extra classes I had taken. After a year of dating, the honeymoon period, my girlfriend and I began to bicker a lot over our differing belief systems. She was a cradle Catholic. I was Sacramentalized but not practicing; I claimed atheism and pursued hedonism. I had left the Church as a young teenager with little resistance from my parents.

My whole family had essentially given up on the faith partly because my older sister, and only sibling, was born with a brain tumor that required multiple surgeries and extensive attention. It wrecked my family financially, emotionally, and spiritually. It was grueling. By the age of four, she was blind because of a procedure. When she was just five, she underwent severe radiation, which was rare for a child at that time. Rather than embrace God, my parents and extended family were mad at God over my sister's condition.

Thankfully, my family has returned to the Church despite years of anger over my sister's misfortune and the fact that she could not enjoy growing up like a "normal" child. Those challenges, however, did not stop my sister from becoming the most joyful and loving person I know. Today, my sister is a chef and caterer. Her success landed her in *Ripley's Believe It or Not*. She has touched the hearts of so many with her story of joy, hardship, and perseverance. I have never met someone who loves better than my sister.

The goal of life is to learn how to love, that's what I learned from the Christian theologians I read to build my case against God when I was dating my wife. I was intensely arrogant and overly confident she could not combat my intelligence, so I read up on all the atheist authors I had admired: Sam Harris, Christopher Hitchens, Richard Dawkins, Daniel Dennett, and classics like Nietzsche and Freud. I wanted to share with her what all the intellects said about God, but I felt there was something lacking even though they were smart and articulate. To gain a greater advantage, I then decided to read classic Christian philosophers like G.K. Chesterton, C.S. Lewis, St. Augustine, St. Thomas Aquinas, and more. I read with the intention of poking holes in their arguments, but my aim backfired. I unwittingly became philosophically trained. I didn't know these were the best of the best until I started comparing them to the atheists I had studied. Slowly and steadily, I found myself becoming more agreeable to the Christian position.

Still, I did not enter a personal relationship with Christ. I remained emotionally reluctant, which twisted me into painful knots over time. About midway through my NBA career, I could no longer stomach the tension within myself caused by what I knew to be true and how I felt about what I knew. I did not want to "go all in" for fear of what my life might look like and the difficulty associated with my misperception. When I couldn't take the inner turmoil any longer, I literally got down on my knees and began to pray, perhaps for the first time in my life. Then I started reading the bible to learn and listen, rather than to form an argument against it.

At 17, the NBA was my dream job, but it became the job from hell when my moral convictions took over. As I adopted a Christian worldview and embraced Jesus Christ as Lord, I began to loathe my career. I felt I could no longer work for an organization that took substantial amounts of money from a Communist country that enslaves an entire ethnic group, the Uyghurs, violates its own citizens' human rights, and abuses children. In addition to the "where the money is coming from" problem, I felt the NBA was an in-your-face idol-making factory. The kids and adults I saw at Jr. NBA events and All-Star weekends truly worshiped the players the NBA promoted at every turn.

Financially, my family was in good shape because, in addition to my job, I understood the stock market and played it well. My wife was able to stay home to raise our children. At once I realized, however, that both sources of our family's income were corrupt, and I knew what I had to do. I felt as though the stock market was salvageable, so I quit the NBA and with my wife's blessing, I invested what savings we had in the development of a website that would pick stocks on a moral basis. It was an ethical stock screener. After a few months of turning a profit, I realized my software only vetted individual stocks, not the stock market as a whole.

God put it on my heart that the whole of the stock market produces too much evil (the subject of this book), so I converted my website to a non-profit dedicated to the theology of money and the relationship Christians should have with wealth. While my non-profit met the goal of educating fellow Christians, it was not a source of sustainable income. With three children and a fourth on the way, my wife and I prayed about what we could do to provide for our young and growing family.

One night, she encouraged me to get out with some friends, sensing I needed a release from all the pressure. While I was out, I received a call from a large parish in need of a bookkeeper. I thought the position might be junior to my experience, including the compensation, so I agreed to help out only temporarily. After arriving at the parish, I was introduced to the enormity of its campus, which included two school buildings, two cemeteries, three churches, and much more. They didn't need a bookkeeper; they needed a business operations manager. When a neighboring school saw how I turned the parish ledger from red to black, they brought me in to help, and then a third ministry did the same. Before I knew it, I was gainfully employed again. God restored everything I had lost in my effort to follow Him and rewarded me for my obedience.

I do not subscribe to the prosperity gospel idea, but I do believe in God's providence. The prosperity gospel relies on human will rather than God's will because it promotes manifesting results through positive thoughts. Advocating for positive thought is good but it's not complete without total consecration to the Sacred Heart of Jesus. It is His will, not ours. This life is about building treasure in heaven not on earth, yet he can always be relied upon to provide what is needed.

I was skeptical and somewhat fearful as I dove into my Catholic faith but educating myself about it left no doubt that taking the leap and trusting God was the only way to go. I share this because as you read, you may experience the same internal tug of war that I felt. Please let my experience serve as just one of the plethora of witnesses to God's glory. Consider Jesus' call to his apostles and other disciples. He simply said, "follow me." He also told many that their faith had saved them. This realization coupled with prayerful reflection helped me overcome my doubt and worry about having to make life adjustments, but I quickly learned that Jesus' yoke really is easy and his burden is light.

Consider the following chapters a proposition, not an imposition.

CHAPTER 2

STOCK MARKET HISTORY

The first stock exchange was created in Amsterdam in 1611 by the Dutch East India Company, which had started selling shares to private investors almost a decade earlier in 1602. However, it should be noted that although speculative buying of goods has been in existence for almost all of documented human history, the introduction of an exchange was something new.

By sovereign law, the Dutch East India Company was a monopoly that held control over several islands near Thailand (modern day Singapore, Hong Kong, Macau, Timor), especially involving the importation of spices that could be found in that area of the world. Effectively, investors bought shares of trading voyages to the East Indies, thus financing the endeavor. If the voyage turned a profit, the purchasers reaped a "sharing" of the proceeds. These investments were risky due to shipwrecks, piracy, or failure to bring back sufficient goods.

The Dutch East India Company eventually learned that many people would not buy shares because profits from the often years-long voyages could not be gained until after the voyage was completed. To address this hesitation, it allowed its shareholders to resell shares on the exchange to other speculators. This enabled investors to gain a profit before the maturity date of the share as long as someone else was willing to pay a higher price for that share than what the original purchaser paid.

By the late 1700s, multiple stock exchanges worldwide consolidated practices due to the Buttonwood Tree Agreement (which became known as the New York Stock Exchange). The Buttonwood Tree Agreement consisted of twenty-four stockbrokers and businessmen on Wall Street in New York City.

The purpose of the agreement was to cut out reckless speculators who were attempting to gain control of the debt securities market, which had caused a financial panic. "How a Financial Panic Helped Launch the New York Stock Exchange," a Time Magazine article,[1] provides more background. By 1896 the Dow Jones Industrial Average had been created. History of its inception can be found in, "Dow Jones Industrial Average First Published," on the Library of Congress website.[2]

In 1926, just three years before the Great Depression, the S&P 500 began tracking and reporting stocks in real time through ticker tape machines enabled by telegraph. Four decades later, in 1971, the NASDAQ (National Association of Securities Dealers Automated Quotations) was created and with it trading became even more commonplace for the retail investor, that is, a private citizen with a brokerage account. Innumerable other indexes were created in the vein of the Dow Jones. Indexes track countless market sectors and subsectors and subsectors of subsectors.

Tax-sheltered retirement accounts such as 401(k)s and Roth IRAs were created in the early 1980s and mid-1990s, respectively. The first Exchange Traded Funds, or ETFs, were created in the 1990s. Essentially ETFs "bundle" securities within specific

---

1 Waxman, Oliva B. "How a Financial Panic Helped Launch the New York Stock Exchange." Time, May 17, 2017, https://time.com/4777959/buttonwood-agreement-stock-exchange/. Accessed March 6, 2024.

2 Library of Congress, Research Guides. "Dow Jones Industrial Average First Published." Library of Congress, https://guides.loc.gov/this-month-in-business-history/may/djia-first-published. Accessed December 17, 2023.

sectors such as tech, government bonds, commodities, utilities, or health care.

These financial tools, along with computers and broker houses, such as Schwab and Edward Jones, allowed the everyday retail investor to instantly invest in markets. In aggregate, the bundling of securities in these various financial instruments allows investors to pay professional managers to manage savings. For most investors in the western world, the primary goal is to accumulate a large amount of savings for consumption during retirement.

A security is any financial instrument that can be traded between parties. In common parlance, the securities held in retirement accounts are marketed as convenient tools to help the little guy get a slice of the massive profits that the fat cats on Wall Street typically accumulate for themselves. However, the 401(k) inventor himself, Ted Benna, has gone on record saying he created a monster. His claim is that the 401(k) has allowed Wall Street to get away with ridiculously high fees hidden beneath layers of financial jargon; the individual is unaware of the true cost. These hidden costs for the typical American household are $155,000 in real dollars over the lifetime of a 401(k). Benna's regret is captured in "Man Who Invented Modern Retirement Issues Warning" by Stock Trading Pro.[3]

Not counted are the true hidden costs of massive consumer debt by the increased purchasing power of conglomerates like BlackRock and Vanguard at exponentially greater rates compared to the purchasing power of retail investors. Similar arguments can be applied to ETFs, which many analysts think have caused increased volatility in the market. The increased volatility is thought to come from the further separation of the actual

3 Stock Trading Pro, Retirement Warning. "Man Who Invented Modern Retirement Issues Warning." Stock Trading Pro, https://stocktradingpro.com/retirement-warning/. Accessed June 1, 2024.

productive activity of a company and investors' investments. It should also be noted that since ETFs are easily accessible to retail investors, who are notoriously bad at investing because their fear of losing money dictates their market activity, the market becomes more susceptible to moving with the emotions of the people, thus causing additional volatility. Some research claims that 76% of retail investors lose money.[4]

This brief history of the market serves two purposes. First, it is good to know how we got to our current situation and second, it is important to understand that the market, as we know it today, is a relatively new human concept. Ignorance is bound to exist in something so new to humanity. This ignorance, rooted in novelty, is one of the reasons why many cannot see the societal ills that the market directly causes.

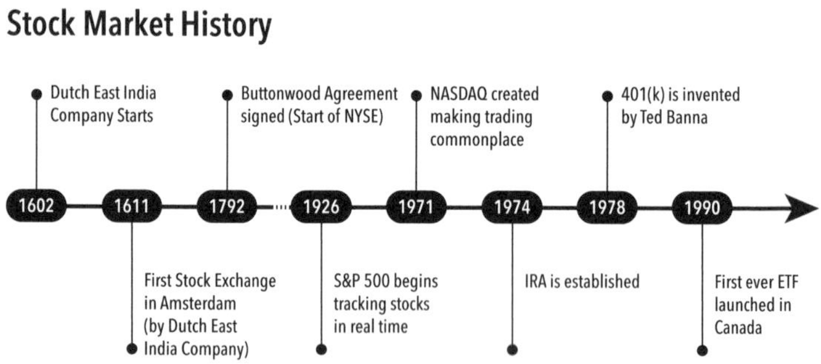

4 Salvucci, Jeremy. "What are retail investors? Definition and market impact." The Street, September 9, 2023, https://www.thestreet.com/dictionary/retail-investors#:~:text=According%20to%20most%20sources%2C%20the,trading%20platform%20for%20the%20statistic. Accessed January 6, 2023.

HOW THE STOCK MARKET WORKS

To understand how the stock market works, we will analyze an individual stock. What happens from the IPO (initial public offering) to the time a retail investor buys or sells a stock? Here is a simplified, step-by-step answer:

1. A company decides to IPO, which means to go public and sell ownership shares of its company to willing parties. The company has a massive monetary incentive to IPO. The amount of cash that comes into a company right after its IPO is game-changing and will usually enable the company to grow exponentially.
2. Wealthy investors, institutional investors, well-connected people, and hedge funds buy up the shares of the newly listed public company. By law, the average everyday investor with a trading app on their phone will most likely never be able to buy these initial share offerings. The SEC (U.S. Securities and Exchange Commission) actually states, "It is often the case that underwriters and dealers will distribute most of the shares in the IPO to their institutional and high net-worth clients, such as mutual funds, hedge funds, pension funds, insurance companies and high net-worth individuals. For the typical investor, being able to directly buy in a popular IPO is a unique opportunity" (Investor Bulletin: Investing in an IPO).[5]
3. The company receives funds from the people who buy the IPO shares and uses that money to grow. This is the first and last time a publicly traded company receives capital from purchasing its stock unless, on a rare occasion, it holds onto some stock for a special second offering.

---

5 Securities and Exchange Commission, Office of Investor Education and Advocacy. "Investing in an IPO." SEC, https://www.sec.gov/files/ipo-investorbulletin.pdf. Accessed June 5, 2023.

4. The wealthy investors who participated in the IPO can sell the stock they purchased from the company to whomever they please, including the general retail investor.
5. Once an initial investor in an IPO sells their stock in a company, the buyer of that stock is not directly supporting the company in any real monetary way. Rather, the buyer is supporting the seller in a direct monetary way. The company receives some indirect benefits from the constant purchasing and selling of its stock on the market in terms of the publicity associated with buying and selling and the opportunity to boost executive compensation packages, which almost always include stock options. Employee stock options, also called equity options, are restricted to the corporation issuing them and are usually guaranteed to rise, thus the benefit, to both the employer and employee, of including these in compensation packages. Equity options on stocks that trade in the market are unrestricted bets that can either fall (puts) or rise (calls).

How the Stock Market Works

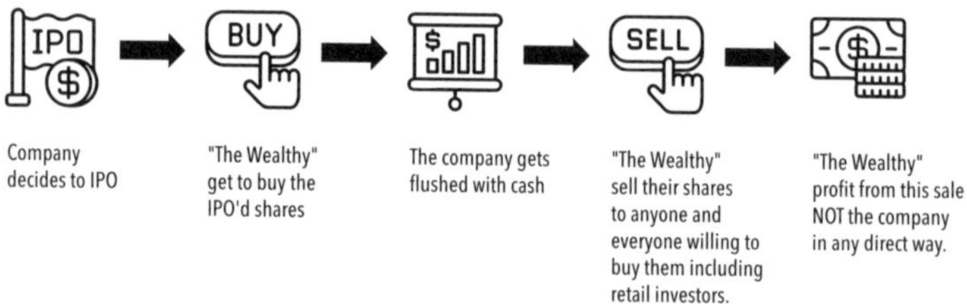

One aspect of the stock market that needs to be addressed and firmly understood before we move on is voting rights.

Voting rights/ownership is a component of the "how-the-stock-market-works" equation that I do not like to harp on as an argument against secondary market investing, yet the basics of both voting rights and traditional Christian social teaching must be grasped before we move on. My fellow crusaders have correctly argued that the voting rights associated with some forms of stock ownership do not qualify as true ownership and thus should not warrant compensation, but in my experience, this argument seems to lack the ability to convince someone of the immorality of the market. This is not to say that these arguments are not valid—I believe they are—but other arguments are more convincing on both intellectual and emotional levels, so we'll focus more heavily on those later on.

Yet, I still feel compelled to state that the Catholic ideal is for each person to own productive property and maintain it. Productive property is property that can be used to produce the necessities of life without impinging upon others. Pope St. John Paul II wrote in his 1991 encyclical, Centesimus Annus, "It is through work that man, using his intelligence and exercising his freedom, succeeds in dominating the earth and making it a fitting home. In this way, he makes part of the earth his own, precisely the part which he has acquired through work; this is the origin of individual property" (#31).

The inherent responsibility that comes from true labor, thus justifying compensation, seems to be absent in stock holding. Sure, stockholders get the right to vote in company board meetings, but they do not have to vote. There is no true work required or responsibility being had when owning a stock. Compensation is just expected, devoid of any responsibility. This would seem to make stockholding an illegitimate form of ownership as it relates to Church teaching.

When you buy a share of a company, you get voting rights that enable you to cast a ballot at the company's board meetings. While this is technically true, it is mostly a façade because only those with massive shareholdings actually get a seat on the board of directors, and that usually ends up being hedge funds or giant investment firms like BlackRock, Vanguard, and State Street.

(Hedge Funds are simply partnerships that invest aggressively in various financial assets using borrowed money.)

Common retail investors typically are not given a meaningful voice; besides, most people do not even own stocks in a way that would allow them to vote in the first place. Bundled investment vehicles like ETFs, 401(k)s, and IRAs do not award the ability to vote to their "owners." Highlighting the façade that is voting rights/ownership, institutional investors own, on average, about 71% of shares in any given company, while everyday retail investors only own about 29% of shares of any given company.[6,7]

Institutional investors routinely vote in company meetings, utilizing almost 90% of the voting rights they possess, while retail investors only use about 25% of the voting rights they possess. Retail investors are only using a quarter of their voting power, and they only own a quarter of the shares to begin with. At best, retail investors have an insignificant voice at company board meetings (Prepping for Proxy Season: A Primer on Proxy Statements and Shareholders' Meetings | FINRA.org).[8]

Proponents of the morality of stock ownership might respond by asserting that every vote counts. However, several questions should be considered. If you're a stockholder, have you ever

6 Brav, Alon, Matthew Cain and Jonathan Zytnick. "Retail Shareholder Participation in the Proxy Process: Monitoring, Engaging, Voting." Finance Working Paper No 637/2019, June 2021, https://www.ecgi.global/sites/default/files/working_papers/documents/bravcainzytnickfinal.pdf. Accessed September 16, 2024.

7 Dore, Kate. "Few individual investors participate in shareholder voting. Here's how that may be changing." CNBC, October 12, 2021, https://www.cnbc.com/2021/10/12/few-individuals-participate-in-shareholder-voting-but-that-may-change.html. Accessed September 16, 2024.

8 FINRA, Investor Insights. "Prepping for Proxy Season: A Primer on Proxy Statements and Shareholders' Meetings." FINRA, February 6, 2023, https://www.finra.org/investors/insights/proxy-season-primer-proxy-statements-and-shareholder-meetings#:~:text=Typically%2C%20somewhere%20between%20a%20quarter,90%20percent%20of%20institutional%20investors. Accessed October 20, 2023.

voted in a company board meeting? If you have voted, was it on anything of substance? Did you purchase the stock so you could vote, or did you purchase the stock in hopes of making a profit? Does your form of stock market investing even allow you to vote? Should voting on something earn you money? Is voting a legitimate form of labor?

Finally, the majority of the stock in any particular company will almost always be held by institutional-type investors. The big players almost never relinquish control of enough stock to the point their voice is not the driving force behind all decision-making. If a retail investor, or any individual, wanted to truly influence a company, the most effective manner would be to simply write a letter as a customer, rather than buying up stock to gain voting rights.

Although we are scratching the surface regarding the function of the stock market, we have covered the basics. These fundamentals make you more knowledgeable about how the stock market works than the vast majority of people investing in it, sadly.

As Christians, we should consider that a stock price is not directly or significantly tied to the production of real goods and services. This is, as will be addressed later in this book, one of the main points that place stock market investing at odds with the Christian ideal. If you were to Google "How is a stock price determined," articles on Investopedia or similar financial education websites would top the search results. Regardless of which article you click, the message will essentially be the same: a stock price is determined by the demand for the stock. You likely will find no information about the actual production of goods and services by the company.

A stock price goes up and down depending on the demand for that stock, and that is it. Yes, price-to-earnings ratios and other financial industry calculations can play a role in the valuation

, but consider this hypothetical example using Tesla. begin to spontaneously combust, shareholders will ir stock, driving down the stock price. Theoretically, if shareholders held onto their Tesla stock and tried to buy more, even while the cars are exploding, the price of the stock would go up, even if consumers stopped purchasing actual Tesla cars.

This concept is demonstrated well by another popular company, Apple. From 2015 to 2020, Apple's operating income hardly changed, yet its market value more than quintupled and its stock price increased from approximately $23.00 to approximately $122.00 per share (Apple Revenue by Year: FY 1990 - 2020 - Dazeinfo).[9] How did this happen? It occurred almost entirely by artificial means, namely, by the company itself buying back $337 billion worth of stock, approximately 30% of its total value. In this scenario, the board and managers of the company had the company itself buy its own stock to drive up the price, which no doubt motivated other investors to get in on the growth and buy Apple stock, accelerating the price increase. These stock price increases had virtually nothing to do with how many phones and computers the company sold.

Instances of stock prices being detached from the production of real goods and services and thus easily manipulated by big players in the market is demonstrated time and time again. Simply research the 2021 AMC Theater and GameStop sagas. The situation in 2021 saw the stock price of two dying companies rise exponentially just because enough people banded together to become a "big player" to manipulate the price of AMC and GameStop stocks. Some statistics support the idea that 75% of economic production that the world economy has experienced in the last few decades has been abstract, not real. This is almost entirely the fault of speculative buying and investing like that

9 Daze Info. "Apple Revenue by Year: FY 1990- 2020." Daze Info, July 28, 2021, https://dazeinfo.com/2019/08/01/apple-revenue-by-year-worldwide-graphfarm/. Accessed October 28, 2023.

which takes place in the stock market. Consider the excerpt below from the National Bureau of Economic Research.

> From 1989 to 2017, $34 trillion of real equity wealth (2017: Q4 dollars) was created by the U.S. corporate sector. We estimate that 44% of this increase was attributable to a reallocation of rewards to shareholders in a decelerating economy, primarily at the expense of labor compensation. Economic growth accounted for just 25%, followed by a lower risk price (18%), and lower interest rates (14%). The period 1952 to 1988 experienced less than one third of the growth in market equity, but economic growth accounted for more than 100% of it (How the Wealth Was Won: Factors Shares as Market Fundamentals (nber.org)).[10]

Of course, demand for a stock is loosely based on the production of real goods and services, with "loosely" being the operative word here. If Apple starts producing some next-generation smartphones, then you better believe the demand for Apple stock will go up. However, Apple stock could also go up because Elon Musk sends out a social media post that he prefers Apple over Android. The stock price of Apple could skyrocket also because some executive makes a claim (true or not) that Android is having logistical problems in Asia. Some claim the 2021 AMC and GameStop examples are outliers and exceptions, when in fact they demonstrate the actual functions of the stock market being put into practice—namely to manipulate an abstract asset so it will grow, and then mine a profit out of it.

The point is that demand for a stock can increase because of some actual production by the company, but it can also take place because of fear-mongering or pure speculation, and most

10 Greenwald, Daniel L, et al. "How the wealth was won: Factors Shares as Market Fundamentals." National Bureau of Economic Research, April, 2019, https://www.nber.org/system/files/working_papers/w25769/revisions/w25769.rev5.pdf. Accessed April 15, 2023.

of the time the general investor has no idea what factor is actually at play.

To this point, I have alluded to the immoral nature of the stock market, but divorce from real productivity and voting rights not being a legitimate form of labor are only pieces of the puzzle. More convincing arguments relate to what the market has produced and its detrimental effects on the world.

PART II

ARGUMENTS AGAINST THE STOCK MARKET

CHAPTER 3

ABSTRACT DOMINANT ECONOMICS

Have you ever seen a stock? They are not tangible; they exist in the forms of 1s and 0s in computer code. I have nothing personal against binary code, but I think we should be skeptical when society keeps moving closer to the abstract and further from the tangible. We have gone from a gold-backed financial system to a "faith in the U.S. government" system, and we are on the precipice of switching to a completely digital financial system. This ever-increasing chasm between tangible and intangible money leads to increased manipulation of our financial system and control over our lives by the powerful. Bank and civil servant employees in China have already started to get paid in digital yuan, and that money may come with an expiration date if the Chinese Communist Party (CCP) wants its population to increase spending. Our government may be far better than the CCP, but history has proven the covetous nature and moral corruption of power. The trend to move away from the tangible and to place our financial livelihoods into digital form managed by obscenely powerful corporations that promote anti-Christian ideas like abortion, LGBTQ legislation, and racial propaganda is a recipe for disaster.

With 75% of our economic activity in the abstract, the majority of our economy is based on estimations and intangible assets with no direct tie to true production. You do not have to be an economist to deduce that this is a heavily inflated system. That 75% statistic, coupled with the fact that all U.S. economic activity is backed by the U.S. dollar, which is backed by the U.S. government, which is over $30 trillion in debt, spells out an inevitable disaster. The whole world should feel compelled to pray that this abstract house of cards stays afloat and nothing dethrones the U.S. dollar as the king of world currencies (or maybe that demise is exactly what is needed for man to properly reset priorities).

The problems with abstract dominant economics do not end with the ability of nefarious players to easily manipulate the system. Even tangible modern fiat currencies are easily manipulatable. The bigger problem with living more and more in the abstract is that we are divorcing ourselves from God's creation. The more we speculate and invest in the stock market, the less likely we are to engage with the physical world. When we invest in the market, we are naturally taking from our abundance and limiting our ability to interact with our communities in the present. All invested capital in the stock market comes from a place of abundance because we do not invest money that we NEED today. This is a tragedy. As Christians, and certainly Catholics, we should focus on corporal works of mercy, using our abundance to care for the poor, build things, and supply needed services, instead of tying up our wealth in 1s and 0s for personal pleasure in an uncertain future.

OBJECTIONS & RESPONSES

Some of the objections presented in this chapter are frequent rebuttals I receive in my crusade against the stock market, even though they may not relate directly to the topic of abstract dominant economics. Thankfully, most people still recognize the benefit of living in the reality of God's creation.

What if I only invest in good companies because I would like to support them?

Investing in good companies is not wrong but you simply can't do this through the stock market. If you have the chance to come alongside a company that is doing some real good in the world, and you give them working capital to accomplish their mission, labor alongside them, and in return receive compensation for your efforts, then all the power to you! But if you want to support this good company by buying its stock, a couple of issues arise.

The most prevalent issue is that you will not be laboring with this company; therefore, any profit you receive would be ill-gotten, as explained in detail previously.

If you want to support a good company, merely purchasing its stock would be a peculiar way of supporting it. As previously stated, when a retail investor buys the stock of a particular company, he is financially supporting only the other investor who sold it to him. The only time a publicly traded company receives a financial benefit from its stock being purchased is in the initial IPO, and the general retail investor does not get to participate in that process. The best way to support a company is by purchasing its product or service, not its stock. You could also support a company you like by making a favorable social media post, talking it up to friends and family, or even sending the company money directly. Any of these efforts would help the company far more than purchasing its stock on the secondary market.

If a company is publicly traded, then it is in the business of growing for growth's sake. A publicly traded company must appease its shareholders by constantly growing and improving the value shareholders get. The majority shareholders that make up the board of directors are the owners of the company, and they reap a profit only if the stock price increases. The company selling more goods and services can have just an indirect effect on the stock price. The more important thing to the stockholder of a company is that the stock price increases, the tangible success of the company is an afterthought. This is problematic because if sights are set solely on profits and growth, then the human elements of compassion, charity, and overall morality will surely be lost. This is why you see the biggest stocks being attached to some of the most nefarious companies (Microsoft, Apple, Amazon, Bank of America, Meta, and so many others). I, and most of those that support the ideas of this book, agree that simple free market capitalism (THINK: people starting businesses and being free to exchange goods and services, i.e. the primary market not the secondary/stock market) is the best economic system for the common good, but it needs to be governed by a moral code, namely Christianity. I do not support the current form of capitalism, or crony capitalism, as some call it, which gave birth to things like the stock market and is wrought with corruption. Fortunately, decoupling from the stock market is low hanging fruit that we can grasp.

In short, there are better ways to support a company than buying its stock on the secondary market, which only pushes it further down the path of growth for growth's sake and incentivizes the globalization and secularism the market helps to create. These better ways may not line your pockets directly but they are not morally problematic and they will have better effects on the common good. Buying ethically produced goods and services will always be better for an economy, especially a Christian one, as opposed to saving and investing in abstractions.

NOTE: Most of the bigger, more dominant publicly traded companies that make up the average portfolio engage in illicit activities. If this concept is new to you, then I highly suggest you spend time doing some research on one of the following sites: ChristCenteredCapital.com, briinstitute.com, or inspireinsight.com. Each site outlines which companies are opposed to Christian and conservative values. It probably won't surprise you to find out the big stocks that make up your 401(k) along with the best ETFs receive some of the worst ethical ratings from these moral investment research companies.

I am going to buy a stock so my voice can be heard in the shareholder meetings. We must make our voices heard if we want to enact change.

I already touched on the idea that voting rights should not be a justification for purchasing a stock, but let's dig deeper into this objection. The retail investor is historically bad at utilizing his voting rights, plus the retail investor never has enough voting weight to combat the big hedge funds and institutions. If you want to make your voice heard by a publicly traded company, then write a letter, start an activist group, or simply call them. "The customer is always right" is a cliché, but all clichés contain an element of truth.

The bottom line is that trying to justify buying stock and perpetuating the "growing for growth's sake" model by saying you want your voice to be heard is a bad argument. There are many more influential ways to be heard. Buying stock is just a way to reap a profit while attempting to make your voice heard. And, as I keep stating, reaping a profit where you have not labored to produce a good or service for the common good is immoral.

Another consideration regarding the perception of voting rights is that seeking to purchase only those stocks where your voice can be heard eliminates most forms of stock market holdings like ETFs, 401(k)s and passive holdings. You only get voting rights when you invest in individual stocks, and most people own stock via retirement accounts, funds, ETFs, and other assets that do not provide their owners with voting rights.

One more thing to consider is why voting on something should earn you compensation. Sure, offering your expertise to a business could be something worthy of compensation if you are contracted to do so, but this requires three things that the common shareholder does not possess: a voice that can actually be heard and implement change, a true expertise in the field that is being voted on (if what is being voted on is even consequential), and a true and valid contract or verbal agreement that says you are being compensated for your expertise.

I have enough money to purchase a sizable portion of stock in a particular company. If I purchase this stock, I could really make my voice heard and steer the company towards the common good. Receiving potential compensation for this would seem just if I actively exercise my influence.

Admittedly, this is one of the strongest objections on its face, but it only seems strong because it is so unique and impractical and therefore, weak. If you are a billionaire and you want to impose your Christian views on a company that has gone public or is going public by purchasing a large portion of its stock or even a majority of it, then I have just one counter-objection. You are still promoting the stock market as a whole and all its ills (e.g., reaping where one has not sown, growth for growth's sake, greed, sloth, anxiety, family decay, etc.). If you have that kind of capital, then the options are endless as to what you could do to promote the common good. Why would you take those options off the table and put yourself into a position where you would be promoting something that is doing so much harm to the common good?

Taking this scenario further, let's suppose you intend to buy all of the shares and make the company go private. This would be great, but there are only a handful of people in the world who would be able to do this to a publicly traded company. This idea is completely impossible for the vast majority of people for whom this book is written. Plus, this would most likely have a negative effect on your personal wealth, which is the opposite effect stock market investors seek. If you are a person with this kind of influence, power, and conviction … well, I am honored that you would read my book, Mr. Musk! Let's talk.

CHAPTER 4

PREDATORY INFLATION

Inflation is a part of the economic life cycle. The rudimentary definition of inflation is money losing value and/or the price of goods and services increasing. When the demand for food, shelter, and clothing increases, the government is incentivized to print more money, which causes inflation. This type of inflation is typically gradual or transitory; we have become accustomed to it. However, when the government prints additional fiat currency to increase the money supply in circulation just to satisfy the demand for an abstraction like Microsoft stock, it creates a serious problem.

Demanding a stock, something that has the sole purpose of producing more money (i.e., selling it for a profit), is not like demanding a house that has the purpose of shelter or demanding food that has the purpose of nutrition. We are essentially demanding a thing that is designed to produce more money. When we use money to demand more money, the dollar loses value. This is a sin against our neighbor because it raises our purchasing power, thus raising the price of goods and services while adding no value to those goods and services. As a result, our neighbors pay more for things that do not improve their lives in a meaningful way. In fact, higher costs are a detriment to their wellbeing. In other words, we invest in the market for selfish gain, and our neighbor pays the price. In a way, we do too because all of those price hikes hit our wallets as well. Yet, we invest in the market to avoid our dollar losing its value.

We may turn to trading platforms like Robinhood that offer $0 fees on trades, which sounds too good to be true because it is. There is no such thing as a free lunch. How are the middlemen able to provide such a seemingly great service without collecting a fee? There are several answers to this question and they can be somewhat complex, so I will focus on and simplify the basic construct such brokers utilize to make money, which is Payment for Order Flow (PFOF).

Robinhood has a relationship with what are known as market makers (very large financial firms). Market Makers essentially pay Robinhood for rights to the massive trade volume that comes through Robinhood's platform. The market makers get to buy shares at a discount. They see and use "better" prices than what you, the individual investor, sees on your $0 trading app. The market makers then profit off these sales in big ways.

Here is an example of how it works in a nutshell. Again, please note that I am offering a super simplified summary. Let's say 10,000 trades for Apple stock come into Robinhood at $220/share. Robinhood has already made a deal with Market Maker ABC. ABC pays Robinhood a fee of half a penny for each trade (this is a volume game). ABC then buys the shares at Apple's market maker price of $218.50 and sells them to you, the retail trader, at $220. Robinhood makes its profit in fees, ABC makes its profit by selling the traders the stock at an upcharge, and the retail trader is left thinking they got a deal and have moved up in life. Yet, the retail trader has just dug themselves into an even bigger hole by exponentially increasing the purchasing power of the market maker while diminishing their own.

The same thing takes place when a bunch of traders want to sell their Apple stock. Except this time ABC, our market maker, is able to take your sale at an ask price and sell it at a bid price. The bid price is higher than the ask, of course. It is the reverse of what is done during the purchase of a stock.

There are always two prices to a stock. Whether the retail investor is selling or buying, they are doing so at the less advantageous price and the market maker is executing the order at the more advantageous price.

The practice of PFOF is frowned upon by a lot of people and the SEC has passed many laws to regulate it. The UK wants to phase out the practice by 2026, but I am not holding my breath for that.

It is a rigged system. The problem is that if we do not invest our money in the market, then it will most certainly lose its value, because most others are investing in the market. The only perceivable solutions are to either get enough people to stop using the stock market or start producing something and earn money in the present. Now, I know this sounds both bleak and idealistic, but just because the ideal is difficult, does not mean it should not be tried. If the ideal is never the aim, then certainly it will never be reached.

The harsh reality is that even if you are one of the few retail investors that is actually making money on the market, you are still losing. Say you turn $100 into $10,000 over the course of just a few years. You have just helped prop up a system, the stock market, that awards the biggest players like BlackRock and Vanguard at exponentially greater rates than you have been rewarded. "So, what?" you say, you're still $9,900 richer than you would have been. But are you really? If some hedge fund was able to turn $10 million into $100 million at the same time you earned your $9.9K, then even you, one of the rare winners of retail investing, cannot compete with the increased purchasing power of the hedge fund. You and all other retail investors have helped the big players increase their purchasing power at your and your neighbor's expenses. This is why we may have more money than previous generations, depending on how you do the calculations, but we can't afford the things that matter like land.

OBJECTIONS & RESPONSES

If we are hurting our neighbor by investing in the market, then we should just convince them to also invest in the market. This way our neighbor will have an increased purchasing power that is able to deal with the price hikes from inflation.

This objection is a bit far-fetched. Besides, convincing others to do bad things is sinful. Additionally, the inflation-causing stock market system negatively affects the person investing in it, too. The only true financial winners in the stock market casino are people at the top of the totem pole like Elon Musk and Warren Buffet. As billionaires continue to invest in the market, the purchasing power increases for the overall economy but becomes increasingly centralized among particular individuals.

Your $200,000 retirement account or even your multi-million-dollar portfolio cannot keep up with the likes of BlackRock and Berkshire Hathaway. The major whales in the market will always increase their wealth via the market at rates that the everyday person cannot match.

The big-time players investing in the market cause an increase in purchasing power that is centralized, and this increased purchasing power naturally leads to inflation. This type of inflation is caused by a force that does not improve products or services, yet average consumers are forced to pay more for products and services.

For example, imagine investment firm XYZ increases their capital from $100 million to $500 million during the same time frame that your 401(k) increases from $10 thousand to $50 thousand. You cannot use the money in your 401(k) for another 10-20 years, and even if you could, the increase would help you very little if investment firm XYZ took their profits and started buying up farmland and apartment buildings. The acquisition of land by company XYZ has made the cost of land, a limited resource, go up at extraordinarily fast rates. Does this scenario seem familiar? Inflated real estate prices make it more difficult for you to buy a home of your own.

Also, the increase XYZ experienced flooded the economy with more money, thus increasing the purchasing power of the economy as a whole, but in a very centralized way. More money in the economy equals higher prices, i.e., inflation. The worst part about all this is it was not done through natural means, i.e., improving or producing a good or service. Instead, it was done through speculative means that delivered no enhancement on production, and you helped XYZ facilitate this by engaging with the market and giving it more fuel (aka dollars) for the fire. The stock market is a speculative system that ultimately hurts our fellow man because it decreases the value of his dollar while raising the price of the necessities of life.

Bill Gates and Jeff Bezos have bought up massive amounts of farmland recently, inflating real estate prices across the country. This is simple supply and demand economics. Mr. Gates and Mr. Bezos were able to purchase thousands of acres because they used the market to convince people to buy abstractions like stocks. When those stocks ballooned in value, they sold them off and bought truly productive things, namely, land. The rich grow richer in a very tangible way, and the rest of us are stuck holding onto things that are easily manipulated and, in a certain sense, worthless.

CHAPTER 5

A GLOBALIZED FINANCIAL SYSTEM

I think most would agree that the stock market and the exchanges of the world have led us to a more globalized society. I could pick up my phone in Pennsylvania and within seconds invest in a company that is based in the UK. Many people would argue that this is one of the great benefits of the secondary market; it has made us all a bit more connected. It should not come as a surprise that I fundamentally disagree with this sentiment. We may be able to connect with ease but are we truly connected? Certainly not in ways that will help create saints. Our connection through technology makes us more reliant on corporations that we otherwise would not even know existed.

A global society is an isolated society. As we become more global, we continually become more disconnected from our local communities. A global society prefers the convenience of working from home over driving to an office to work alongside others. A global society prefers the convenience of shopping at conglomerates that can deliver goods right to their homes rather than shopping at community-based stores. Intentionally or not, a global society is inclined to invest in big corporations that span the globe rather than investing in local businesses.

Likewise, a global society prefers the ease with which it gets entertainment from big industries in the comfort of home rather than going out and mingling with neighbors. These behaviors isolate us and diminish our ability to love our neighbor because they limit our ability to be with our neighbor. Our local community is the only place where we can get authentic human interaction and commune with others, which of course, is the best way to love another person. This is why I've concluded that a globalized society is an isolated society. Globalization isolates individuals. The stock market and the exchanges of the world have helped cultivate this situation. After all, a company is on the stock market for the sake of growth; to perpetuate growth, bigger companies must become global and create a global society that abets their mission.

When a company goes public, it commits itself to growth for the sake of growth. The board of directors with the most shares are only going to profit if the company continues to grow. Going public draws the eyes of the world toward the company, and its sole focus shifts from producing a high-quality product or service to improving its public perception for the purpose of increasing the stock price and meeting shareholder obligations. It is a marketing over quality approach. Of course, producing a high-quality product or service can help with perception, but this is secondary, not primary. The commitment to growth for growth's sake after going public has contributed to catapulting society to its current globalized state. Apple must expand to China; Tesla must open factories in Germany; and that Virginia-based company that went public must expand into the West and the Northeast areas of the U.S. because if these companies do not do these things, then they are not growing and shareholders are not profiting. Growing for the sake of growth is the name of the game for publicly traded companies, and this leads to a globalized marketplace. A globalized marketplace isolates the individual, and small, local communities suffer because individuals are not as engaged as they should or could be. If communities suffer because of isolated individuals, then so will families. If families suffer, then fewer saints will be produced.

OBJECTIONS & RESPONSES

A globalized world allows us to be connected in a way that has facilitated massive improvements to infrastructure, brought clean water to third-world countries, and allowed those crippled by poverty to reap the economic benefits of richer areas of the world. If the stock market has played a key role in this globalization, then shouldn't we embrace it for these reasons and more?

Yes, the stock market has helped produce a globalized society, and maybe a globalized society has played some role in improving living conditions around the world. I am all for improved living conditions and lifting people out of poverty, but the ends do not justify the means. We should not use something to produce goods if the thing we are using is immoral. We must embrace good means to produce good ends. When we make exceptions, corruption will take over.

Perhaps I have not fully convinced you that society at large is at the bottom of a hill of deterioration and the stock market is at the top. Perhaps you want to embrace the market and its cultivation of a globalized society. Fine. I beseech you, however, to first give serious consideration to all that a globalized society produces, not just the goods. If my theory about a globalized society creating isolated individuals rings true, then you cannot embrace the stock market, no matter how much clean water it indirectly delivers to the poor and sick. Many people in Cuba loved Pablo Escobar for bringing them out of poverty, but does this justify his means of selling drugs and ruining countless lives?

Also ask yourself if proceeds from the stock market are the only means by which we would be able to bring clean water and clothing to the poor. Is the stock market the only tool we have at our disposal that can facilitate care for the poor and the sick? Of course not, we are smart and capable of great charity. We simply need to flex those two muscles.

We do not need the stock market, we need virtue. We knew how to purify water and transport it long before the creation of the stock market, we had missionaries for the sick long before the New York Stock Exchange, and we knew how to build shelter long before the Dutch East India Company came into existence. The materials have been there always; God supplied them in abundance. We simply need to be more charitable with our time, talent, and treasure. If profit is the only motivating factor to do good, then humanity is doomed!

CHAPTER 6

SCRIPTURE AND CHURCH TEACHING

Volumes have been written detailing the relationship between scripture, church writings, speculation, labor, and money. In this chapter, I synthesize my study of these things, proving that Christians should be opposed to the stock market.

Let's first look at Pope St. John Paul II and how he makes the case in his 1991 encyclical Centesimus Annus. The saint commends investing but in two different sections he notes that speculation does not qualify as true investing. He states, "The spread of improper sources of growing rich and of easy profits deriving from illegal or purely speculative activities constitute one of the chief obstacles to development and to the economic order" (48).

I cannot think of anything that fits into the saint's description of easy profits and pure speculation better than the stock market. Pope St. John Paul II also writes:

> Ownership of the means of production ... becomes illegitimate, however, when it is not utilized or when it serves to impede the work of others, in an effort to gain a profit which is not the result of the overall expansion of work and the wealth of society, but rather is the result of ... speculation, or the breaking of solidarity among working people. Ownership of this kind has no justification and represents an abuse in the sight of God and man (43).

John Paul II is driving home the point that no real ownership is present when what is owned is not properly utilized, but instead is used to hinder others and their work. This complements our arguments that stock market investing hurts our neighbors by causing inflation and increasing the purchasing power of big players at exponential rates. John Paul II is painting the picture that speculation, hindering workers, and a lack of true labor makes the ownership of a stock an illegitimate ownership that is appalling to God.

Next, let's consider 2 Thessalonians, where St. Paul condemns speculation:

> For even when we were with you, we gave you this command: if anyone will not work, let him not eat. For we hear that some of you are walking in idleness, not doing any work. Now such persons we command and exhort in the Lord Jesus Christ to do their work in quietness and to earn their own living. Brethren, do not be weary in well-doing. If anyone refuses to obey what we say in this letter, note that man, and have nothing to do with him, that he may be ashamed (2 Thes 3:10–14).

The Greek word that St. Paul uses for not doing any work is the participle of περιεργάζομαι, periergazomai. Dictionaries of ancient Greek say this word literally means to tell others how to buy and sell, or to bargain or haggle (περὶ τῆς τιμῆς) over saleable goods in the market. If these dictionaries are indeed correct, then the apostle hereby makes plain the Christian orientation toward wealth: a person must engage in productive labor in order to deserve his place in the community. My argument that the only way a person should receive compensation is through productive labor that supports the common good seems to be in agreeance with St. Paul.

Returning to Pope St. John Paul II's Centesimus Annus, we get a healthy dose of wisdom:

> Even the decision to invest in one place rather than another, in one productive sector rather than another, is always a moral and cultural choice. Given the utter necessity of certain economic conditions and of political stability, the decision to invest, that is, to offer people an opportunity to make good use of their own labor, is also determined by an attitude of human sympathy and trust in Providence, which reveal the human quality of the person making such decisions (36).

John Paul II teaches us that investing is always a moral decision and one that should be oriented towards the betterment of all, not just the financial gain of one. When we invest, we should be giving others the chance to work and start businesses that can also be productive for the common good. The stock market is something that not only hinders our neighbor, as I have argued, but also fails to give our fellow man an opportunity to engage in this productive work or start businesses, which JPII claims is a prerequisite to good investing.

Our Lord is not silent on this issue either. In Luke Chapter 16, Christ shares much wisdom about money matters. Chief among them is when He says, "And I tell you, make friends for yourselves by means of unrighteous mammon, so that when it fails, they may receive you into the eternal habitations" (Lk 16:9). Making use of our wealth for the betterment of all is something about which our Lord, John Paul II, and many others in good standing with our Lord agree.

I have laid out the case that stock market investing does not better all but hurts our neighbors, who we should love, in the shameful name of profits.

Matthew 6:19-20 is powerful and direct: "Do not lay up for yourselves treasures on earth ... lay up for yourselves treasures in heaven." None of us knows the hour of his death; the time we spend amassing riches to be used later is time taken from loving our neighbor. Our Lord is telling us in a direct way to be focused on the eternal future, not our retirement. Just think about how in Luke Chapter 12, our Lord calls the rich man who yielded an abundant harvest a fool for storing his surplus.

We should reflect on the parable of the rich fool when discerning the truth about the stock market. Read it in full then pause for a moment to digest these words of our Lord.

> And he told them a parable, saying, "The land of a rich man brought forth plentifully; and he thought to himself, 'What shall I do, for I have nowhere to store my crops?' And he said, 'I will do this: I will pull down my barns, and build larger ones; and there I will store all my grain and my goods. And I will say to my soul, Soul, you have ample goods laid up for many years; take your ease, eat, drink, be merry.' But God said to him, 'Fool! This night your soul is required of you; and the things you have prepared, whose will they be?' So is he who lays up treasure for himself, and is not rich toward God" (Lk 12:16-21).

In Ezekiel 18:5-9 the prophet gives us a prescription for what the righteous and lawful ought to do. "If a man is righteous and does what is lawful and right, … does not lend at interest or take any increase, withholds his hand from iniquity, … he is righteous, he shall surely live, says the Lord God." Ezekiel's condemnation of the practice of usury and warning against ill-gotten increase can easily correlate to the stock market.

In Luke 6:34-35 Our Lord Jesus Christ says, "And if you lend to those from whom you hope to receive, what credit is that to you? Even sinners lend to sinners, to receive as much again. But love your enemies, and do good, and lend, expecting nothing in return; and your reward will be great, and you will be sons of the

Most High; for he is kind to the ungrateful and the selfish." Our Lord clearly states that it is better to give and expect nothing in return. Most Christians agree on this point, but we operate under the false premise that this is to be done only in rare circumstances, mistakenly thinking Jesus wanted us to do this once in a while, when in reality, Jesus proclaims that this is how we ought to live every day.

I recognize that I fall short of living my life this way, and that I need more grace than I could ever realize this side of eternity. I also believe that in tying up our abundances for the sake of future profits, the stock market practically forces us to live counter to the teachings of our Lord, as directed in chapter 6 of Luke's Gospel.

Consider the simple and profound insights of St. Thomas Aquinas who says the act of making money from money is "unjust in itself" (secundum se iniustum) and "evil simply" (malum simpliciter). The stock market uses money to demand more money. It does not produce tangible goods. Sure, the nature of money has changed since St. Thomas' time, but this is not a convincing reason to dismiss the author of the Summa Theologica, as I demonstrate in Chapter 7, Greed, Sloth, and Other Vices.

OBJECTIONS & RESPONSES

The market is a product of capitalism; outlawing the market would push us closer to socialism or communism which is condemned by the Church.

There are a couple of points to make here. First, choosing to labor and not reap where you have not sown is virtuous, and virtues are tricky to enforce through government law. Vices such as murder, rape, and theft should be outlawed in any civilized society, but virtues are almost impossible to mandate and enforce. Imagine trying to police prohibition in an attempt to make the virtue of temperance a law. It is possible to enforce a law that promotes a virtue, but my penchant toward libertarianism is fueled when I think about the capabilities of the government. Also, virtue becomes more pervasive in society when people choose it freely. I would ally with efforts to get the Church to directly call stock market investing sinful, but I prefer governmental authorities stay out of the conversation because I am not convinced that they would get it right given the level of corruption and incompetence associated with government agencies. That's too bad, too, because I could see myself supporting a well-orchestrated plan to cast out the market from civilized society.

Second, I am a huge proponent of capitalism over socialism and communism, but there is a caveat. The current form of capitalism we practice (which favors corporatism) is only better than the obvious condemned alternatives, and just being better than condemned alternatives does not make something sufficient and morally good. A capitalistic economic environment centered around Christian virtue and Catholic social teaching is where the best of mankind will likely be found.

If capitalism is simply making as much money as possible no matter the cost, then I am out. The fictional Gordon Gekko was wrong when he said, "Greed is good!" On the other hand, if your idea of capitalism is working hard and earning a just wage for your labor because you produced something that promotes the common good of society, then I am 100% in your corner. Basically, a relatively free market society that is governed by the Judeo-Christian ethic should be our goal.

Saint John Paul II wrote extensively about capitalism, socialism, and communism. Make no mistake about it, he opposed all three to some degree. Read his papal encyclicals Centesimus Annus or Laborem Exercens. Of course, he spoke out more noticeably about the evil of his time, namely Marxist collectivism, than he did capitalism. But this does not mean that John Paul II or the Church, in general, are big proponents of capitalism in its current state. Ayn Rand fanboys should not be found within the confines of the Church, either. Ayn Rand, somewhat of a contemporary of John Paul II, is a 20th-century philosopher who was an atheist and promoted the ideals of complete and unfettered self-interest being the highest good. She is most known for her 1957 book *Atlas Shrugged,* where the idea of laissez-faire capitalism is heavily promoted.

Okay, if the stock market is so terrible, then why has the Church not explicitly condemned it? The Church itself even holds stocks!

While the stock market has existed for the entirety of most of our lives, relative to the Church, the stock market is new, and its intricacies are well-known to only a few. The stock market, as it is used today, has existed for just over 40 years, when paired with the creation of the 401(k). Four decades is simply not enough time to learn all the ins and outs of an entity that is constantly evolving and growing ever larger, unless it is your full-time job and passion. Our understaffed Church is focused primarily on administering the sacraments to its people and spreading the Gospel. I'm not making excuses for Church leaders but pointing out the seemingly obvious. Church leaders are trained in theology, not finance, and have little bandwidth to learn the world's economic landscape like a financial analyst would. It appears the market is not an issue Church leaders are prepared to speak about in absolute terms … yet. With help from the laity, perhaps they will become conversant enough to spread the word.

In many ways the Church has spoken out against elements that make up the market. Speculation has been condemned, sloth and greed are two of the seven deadly sins, numerous passages in scripture speak well of true labor and ill of wealth gained without labor, and more than a couple of popes have written about the morality of investing. I believe the most prominent and relevant of these excerpts from scripture and church teaching are those outlined at the beginning of this chapter.

The Church may not have said verbatim, "the stock market is condemned," but it has given us plenty of reasons to be skeptical of the market and how it operates. Given all with which the Church is tasked, plus the relative newness of the secondary market, it is easy to understand why the Church has not explicitly condemned the market and is even a willing participant in it. Our Mother Church deserves grace and charity when appropriate, and we should all be praying for definitive teaching on this subject to come sooner rather than later.

Even if we table the argument about the immorality of the stock market, it is worth noting that parishes, priests, bishops, and dioceses undoubtedly and unwittingly own stock in particularly nefarious companies. The Church's actions are not automatically good simply because it is the Church. Throughout Christianity, many depraved and heinous acts have been committed by the Church and its leadership, but that does not mean that these things have become good, nor does it mean that the Church is not an authoritative voice for the faithful. What it means is that man is flawed and even our popes, cardinals, and bishops are not without sin and mistake. The authority that the Church holds on faith and morals was given by our Lord. The Church that Jesus established when he made St. Peter the first pope accurately interprets scripture and teaches theology. Mistakes regarding how to interact with the world, however, will surely persist until the end of days because we are human. We just need to continually pray to the Holy Spirit for guidance and be sure that we are pursuing our Heavenly Father's will and not our own.

In this objection, and throughout this book, I represent a Catholic perspective, but my Protestant and Eastern Orthodox brothers and sisters should not feel left out. This line of reasoning applies to your parishes and churches as well. For example, if you have a pastor who is an amazing preacher and interpreter of scripture, but it is found out to have beaten his children or been involved in some sort of sexual scandal, does this mean his interpretations are null or his sermons are bad? Emotionally, you may be tempted to say, "yes, his teachings were wrong," but such an emotional response would be throwing the baby out with the bathwater. If someone says God is a trinity, then does something nefarious, it does not mean that what he said about God being a trinity is false; it only means what he did was wrong. If your church invests in the stock market, it doesn't mean you should find a new church. It doesn't mean your pastor's sermon last Sunday was riddled with heresy or that the church finance manager is going to Hell. It indicates that the Devil is deceptive and the market is new and unknown, and we should be praying to discern all new innovations our world has to offer.

What about the parable of the talents in the Gospels of Matthew and Luke? Don't these words from our Lord suggest that it is okay to earn interest and invest in such a way that allows us to reap where we have not sown?

A great essay explaining this parable in detail was written by a friend of mine, Jacob Imam, titled "Rereading the Parable of the Minas." It can be found on his site, newpolity.com,[11] or in the New Polity journal. I strongly urge you to check it out for a more detailed explanation of why the parable should not be interpreted as our Lord's endorsement of reaping where you have not sown.

In the parable, each of three servants is given money, talents, from their master. The first and second double the talents given to them, ten and five respectively. The third servant buries the one talent he was given and then returns it to his master saying, "Master, I knew you to be a hard man (sklēros), reaping where you did not sow, and gathering where you did not winnow" (Mt 25:24). The word "hard man" in Greek is the same as the prefix (sklēros) of the word "hardhearted" (sklēro-kardian). It

11 Imam, Jacob. "Rereading the Parable of the Minas." Newpolity, https://newpolity.com/blog/the-parable-of-the-minas?rq=Rereading%20the%20Parable%20of%20the%20Minas. Accessed December 15, 2023

was because of this hardheartedness (sklēro-kardian) that Moses gave the Israelites the allowance for divorce. Christ is likening usury to divorce in terms of the severity of heart that is required to do either. In the Old Testament Moses permits the ancient Israelites to charge interest on loans to foreigners and allows them to divorce. In the New Testament it seems that Jesus is saying both are products of human sinfulness.

Jesus makes a point to tell the servant that he will be condemned by his own mouth. The parable in Luke's Gospel reads, "I will condemn you out of your own mouth, you wicked servant! You knew that I was a severe man, taking up what I did not lay down and reaping what I did not sow? Why then did you not put my money into the bank, and at my coming, I should have collected it with interest?" (Lk 19:22-23). Jesus is of course the rich nobleman in the parable who has received his kingdom, and we know that Jesus is not a hard man or a thief. Yet, he makes the point that if you believe your Lord to be a thief, then you will become wicked or lazy, or both.

We must know the true Christ if we are to conduct ourselves properly in the world. The parable of the talents is a condemnation of laziness and the act of projecting our own wickedness onto our Lord, not a stamp of approval for reaping where one has not sown. It also should be noted that the rich nobleman in the parable does not ask for his money back from any of his servants, and instead gives them more responsibility. This is a representation of the gift economy that Christ will have in his kingdom.

You say that the only way a person should receive compensation is if they do true labor, but what if you have been gifted money or some rare family heirloom that museums want to pay you for? If receiving money in these situations is justified, then stock market investing should be as well.

Receiving property, cars, other goods, or money from someone is not compensation, it is a gift, and there is nothing wrong with receiving a gift. The money received from trading on the stock market is obviously not in the same category as receiving a generous gift. One is an abstraction that promotes mass speculation and societal ills while the other is the manifestation of charity, the principal Christian virtue.

The other part of this objection requires a bit more flushing out. Say you were gifted a set of rare gold coins from a deceased uncle and a museum curator wants to pay you a monthly fee to put these coins on display. You have hit the jackpot because the coins are so rare that the monthly fee is significant and the coins being pure gold require no maintenance by you. Looks like you are earning compensation for doing no work. According to this book that seems to be immoral.

I believe my core premise, that we ought only to receive compensation when we labor to produce a good or service that promotes the common good excludes the stock market but includes the rare coin example. My premise requires three conditions be met.

1. Labor is being done.
2. A good or service is being produced.
3. The good or service produced promotes the common good.

In the rare coin example, all three criteria are met. Labor has been done in either securing the coins, protecting the coins from theft, maintaining the coins if they are not pure gold, and at the very least managing the coins for sale or rent. The second criterion is also met in that the museum curator or private purchaser are obtaining something of historical significance, monetary value, and/or allowing others to view a beautiful and unique object. Finally, the third criterion is hypothetically met as long as the coins are not intentionally promoting some kind of heresy or the occult but are in fact promoting the good by being a thing of beauty put on display or being used as a valuable commodity to further the good of a person or community.

In contrast, I do not think that secondary market investing meets all three criteria. I am even tempted to say it does not meet any of the three criteria. But alas, for the sake of argument, I concede the point that "work" in the scientific sense of expelling energy is being done when you invest in the market. It may be a lesser form of work than timber framing a barn, but just because something is easy or simple does not mean it is not a kind of work. The simple fry-cook or call switcher is due his wages just like the master carpenter is due his.

I know personally how strenuous it can be to pour over balance sheets and financial articles in the hunt for a lucrative stock or ETF. The real issue of why I personally would not qualify the purchasing of a stock as work is because the three criteria listed above are inextricably linked and you cannot have the first criterion met if you do not meet the other two as well. True labor must end with the promotion of the common good. The second criterion of a good being produced is even more of a stretch since the stock is an abstraction and not a thing of any real utility, which is why I do not think it qualifies as a good. However, even if the first two criteria are conceded, the third criterion is where I want to stand firm. The stock purchase may be a low form of labor, and it may technically qualify as a good to some, but it certainly does not promote the common good, hence the main premise of this book.

The reason the coin example at first glance seems to undermine my argument about true labor is because it is not scalable like the limitless abstract secondary market. If everyone could get their hands on unique coins, then the coins would no longer be unique and therefore worthless. This is not the case with stocks. They can be split and multiplied to infinity, and this is why it promotes mass speculation where the name of the game is not a quality product or service but growth for the sake of growth. If stocks were limited and had systems or laws in place that deterred the greedy from becoming monopolistic, then perhaps that would be something morally licit, but what I just described runs completely counter to what the stock market is. Limiting abstractions and tying them to labor that promotes the common good is an impossibility in our world as we know it.

CHAPTER 7

GREED, SLOTH, AND OTHER VICES

Despite all the good my detractors may think the stock market has done, the fact remains that the market has led us to believe, whether consciously or subconsciously, that greed is good. I once was a huge fan of the movie *Wall Street*, and the main character Gordon Gekko's famous line "Greed is Good," but when I became a Christian, I realized just how perverse that way of thinking is. The stock market offers us a chance to buy low and sell high without any work that benefits our fellow man. This is a big problem! The key to why this is a problem lies within our fallen human nature. Oh, that cursed piece of fruit! We, as the human race, are naturally inclined to pursue the flesh over the spirit. This is why pornography, idol worship of celebrities, and materialism are running amuck through civilization.

We tend to pursue the perverted because of our fallen nature, which makes restraining ourselves a challenge. Therefore, we need to put mechanisms in place that help us stay on the straight and narrow path, which God promises will lead us to salvation. Personal habits like daily prayer and fasting and societal movements like feeding the poor and educating about the negative consequences of abortion can help us stay the course, but one of the most important things we can do is learn what the *good* is and do our best to pursue it.

When we purchase stock market securities, we do so with the sole intention of buying low and selling high for a profit. This form of speculative activity divorces profit from true productive labor by offering us a means to make money by merely selling without adding value to the thing we are selling. As individual investors, we clearly see that it is possible to buy things and later sell them for profit without adding value to them, regardless of what macroeconomic benefits may result from the purchase and sale of a stock. This type of activity has led to vices like greed and sloth.

My claim is tough to put into a nice statistical data point, but there's no denying the relationship between how we invest our resources—time, talent, treasure—and who we become. If we spend our time caring for the poor, we may very well become a saint. Conversely, if we spend our time chasing profits by selling no value-added abstractions, we may very well become greedy. If we are overcome by greed and sloth, other vices are sure to follow. If enough of us are taken over by vices of the flesh, our families and communities will soon follow the same path. We know, however, that because we are all deeply connected, we as individuals can lead the way for our larger Christian family.

Simply put, reaping where we have not sown will make us greedy. Greed is the inordinate love for riches. It makes the acquisition of money and possessions a purpose for living unto itself. When we become greedy, other vices creep into and take over our lives. When one of us gives into sin, others are more likely to do the same. Sin has a ripple effect. For example, if I decide to sell guns on the black market, which is obviously sinful, I am tempting others to sin through this activity. Sin is contagious just like kindness is contagious. If we spend enough time around a truly loving person, we may become more loving ourselves. On the other hand, if we spend enough time around a greedy or slothful person, we too may develop those tendencies. We are products of our environment, that is human nature.

The stock market is reaping where we have not sown because it is allowing us to profit without the obligation to perform value-adding labor. If our goal is to produce saints and bring glory to God, then we cannot divorce compensation from true labor because it will cultivate an environment where our base passions of greed and sloth will surely flourish.

OBJECTIONS & RESPONSES

The Market is one of the factors that has lifted so many people out of poverty and provided us with economic abundance, jobs, and purchasing power. This should not be done away with.

The ends can never justify the means. This is a foundational Christian teaching that must be adhered by all members of the Body of Christ. This means that even if the market produces some good things, directly or indirectly, we cannot participate in it if, as a whole, it is morally wrong.

When we begin to adopt the idea that the ends can justify the means, we are adopting a totalitarian ethic, and this always leads humanity down a depraved path. Just because something has a perceived positive outcome does not mean we should embrace it. Producing pornography can make a lot of money that could be used to fund a crisis pregnancy center, but that does not make producing pornography morally acceptable. Therefore, if it is wrong to participate in the stock market because it cultivates vices and other societal ills as I claim, then it doesn't matter how much money or benefit it provides. A Christian cannot use an evil means to justify a good end.

Also, the idea that the market has produced much economic abundance needs some clarification. I am all for people being lifted out of poverty, but at what cost? Yes, it is true that in the U.S. we have experienced a lot of economic abundance, and the stock market *may* be one of the reasons for this abundance. We have easier access to phones, computers, cars, and clothes than ever before. Many who live below the poverty line are overweight, which is an economic wonder, yet we must question whether such self-indulgent materialism is the economic abundance we, as the Body of Christ, should pursue. Does it produce more saints?

In the West, we as individuals have many possessions yet few of us own homes, land, or productive property. We have sacrificed true independence for comfort, which arguably has made us more manipulable by the market and monopolistic corporations.

At the beginning of 2003, the national consumer debt was $7.23 trillion; at the time of this writing, it is nearly $18 trillion. We have more things, yet we are evermore beholden to financial institutions and major companies. It's as if the stuff we've accumulated has become our tether to corporatocracy. The economic ideal we should pursue as the body of Christ is family-flourishing, which keeps the dignity of the individual intact through meaningful labor, rather than debt-amassing materialism via abstract speculation that puts us into an intellectual and financial stupor.

Another crucial point to consider is what the stock market has produced. As I stated previously, most of our economic growth has been in the abstract over the last several decades. The industrial revolution gets bragging rights for producing most of the new things we experienced in the 20th century and for taking huge portions of the world population out of poverty. The stock market was just the vehicle that many of those producers of the new things used to grow and become monopolistic. If the existence of the stock market really has caused 75% of economic growth to be in the abstract, then what would our economy look like if we didn't have the stock market? Would we live in poverty, or would we be more incentivized to produce necessary and possibly new goods and services?

There are many factors in today's world that cause us to be materialistic, and it is unfair to put the blame entirely on the stock market. Yet it would be a mistake to let the stock market off scot-free. After all, the stock market is responsible for the exponential growth of entities like social media, apparel, automotive, and luxury goods producers purely for the sake of profit. As humans, we are inclined towards greed and sloth, so if we are able to profit simply by purchasing and reselling without performing true labor, what result can we expect? The stock market and its inflation-causing system of demanding abstractions is a key reason why our levels of greed and sloth continue to rise along with our debt.

From where are you getting this premise? Why is laboring to produce a good or service that promotes the common good the only way a person should receive compensation?

Simply put, laboring to produce a good or service that promotes the common good is in alignment with charity and will help us get into heaven. Let's unpack this. Consider the negative effects that may befall an able-bodied person who does not labor but receives money. What do you think will likely happen to that person's character, life, soul, and community? If a capable person can eat and drink and be clothed and sheltered without ever having to lift a finger, is this ultimately a good thing or will that person end up being the adult version of a spoiled brat? Even in the Garden of Eden before the fall of man there was labor to be done, such as naming the animals.

To my knowledge, there is no scripture verse, papal encyclical, or official church document that directly states, "laboring to produce a good or service that promotes the common good is the only way a person should receive compensation." However, a well-formed Christian conscience could easily reason its way to this conclusion. Also, we can parse together many different official church writings and scripture verses to make the case, which we do in subsequent chapters. For now, let's lay out some hypothetical examples to make the case.

Imagine a hitman for hire who makes a good living killing people. His job requires a lot of skill and hard work, and he is compensated well. Would such a job be morally permissible for a Christian? Of course not, because we believe murdering people does not promote the common good. Imagine a scientist who works for a pharmaceutical company that produces abortion pills. Would this person's role be in keeping with Christian morality? Not a chance! Through these examples, we see that simply providing a service or a product does not justify receiving compensation, according to Christian teaching. We also know that if no product or service is provided by an individual, there is very little chance that he will be compensated (trust funds and similar circumstances aside).

To justify any means of compensation, we must provide a product or service that promotes the common good. I do not believe the stock market meets either of these requirements, much less both. My stock market and usury debate opponents attempt to justify their positions by saying they are, in fact, providing a service that promotes the common good because the money generated through trading and lending is a source of livelihood for many. Stipulations on how and when it is acceptable to receive compensation are rooted in our God-given human reasoning ability. The point of contention is whether stock market investing produces things that support the common good. I believe the stock market produces nothing of value and that it negatively impacts the common good because it promotes a culture of reaping where we have not sown (i.e., speculative behavior where profits can be made without productive work).

Again, even if the stock market produces additional income, jobs, and other items that are beneficial to the common good, it is paramount that we do not sacrifice our souls for these goods. For if we come about good things through a method that also promotes vices, then those goods are ill-gotten and worthless. There are many ways to create jobs, put food on tables, and bring people out of poverty, but the methods we pursue must be moral ones. We cannot embrace the market, ignoring its depravities, because of the few good effects it has no more than we can embrace drug cartels and ignore their depravities just because they bring some people out of poverty.

Why is investing in the stock market not considered labor? Researching assets for investment should be considered work.

In the secular sense, work is absolutely being done when a savvy investor purchases a stock. I have combed through enough financial statements, balance sheets, and investment analysis articles to know that this can be hard and stressful work. However, this is a moot point when compared to true labor, as defined previously. True labor is when a service or product is produced that promotes the common good. Although stock market investing can be arduous, it does not align with the Christian definition of true labor.

While stock research can be difficult, the very nature of it is selfish. Profits come at the cost of inflation to our neighbors who lose when our purchasing power increases through the buying and selling of an abstraction that requires no productive labor on our part. Refer to Chapter 4 for a deeper dive into inflation.

Money is no longer a stagnant thing like in the Middle Ages; it is a productive thing. Therefore, why is it wrong to put my money to work in the stock market if I previously earned it through productive labor?

It is true that the nature of money has changed, or at least how we use it has changed, thus making us think it is a productive asset if invested well (I'm addressing the financial aspect, not the moral aspect). This change of perspective should not be accepted blindly. Just because the ideas surrounding something have changed does not mean that it is in keeping with Christian morality. St. Augustine said, "Right is right even if no one is doing it; wrong is wrong even if everyone is doing it." While many Christians have vacillated on issues permeating society, such as the hook-up culture, IVF, and abortion, most understand the arguments in light of St. Augustine's quote yet we rarely, if ever, question or debate what has become a common perception about the exchange of money.

The idea of money being a productive asset is one of my biggest concerns with the current financial industry. At its base, the function of money producing money is inflation, thus the reason debt, housing prices, and the prices of cars, eggs, meat, and raw materials have skyrocketed. The market gives us the chance to earn a living without doing any real labor, and this has made us selfish, money hungry, and lazy. Of course, we are already each of those things because of that pesky thing called original sin, but the accepted concept of having our "money work for us," rather than engaging in true labor has certainly not helped our situation.

Comparing the market to our cultures' avoidance of child-rearing is a dramatization that drives the point home quite well. The ability to engage in sex without the possibility of having to raise a child because of contraceptives and abortion has led to sexual depravity in society. The ability to make profits without performing productive labor has led to financial depravity and all the sin and vice that come with it. The key difference here between sexual depravity and the stock market is that the stock market is a system that is practically forced upon us, whereas we still have freedom to choose to not participate in depraved sexual behavior.

When the profits are divorced from true productive labor, then vices and sin are given the opportunity to creep in. This point is crucial, and worth repeating. We should only receive compensation when we produce something for the common good. If we ignore this stipulation regarding compensation, then we may do so out of greed and sloth, and those same vices will become our masters. No Christian thinks it is okay to use stored labor to produce pornography or start an abortion clinic, so why would we think it is okay to use our stored labor to invest in the stock market?

Note that productive work done in the past does not entitle us to compensation now. Imagine you composed a song years ago—true labor—and you continue to receive royalties from people who purchase your music, your compensation is justified. You are receiving money for producing a great service. If, however, I compose a song and invest the money I earned from it in the market, then I have divorced my initial product or service, the song, from the profits I am currently making in the market.

CHAPTER 8

FAMILY DECAY AND RETIREMENT

The stock market and much of modern-day finance have led to the decay of the family. Once upon a time, we would go to our parents, grandparents, aunts, uncles, and siblings if we needed to buy a home for our family. Now we go to the bank. We used to rely on family to take care of us in our old age, and now we rely on BlackRock and Vanguard. This shift in financial reliance comes under the guise of financial independence, but really, we are always dependent on others financially. We have just made the choice to shift that dependence from the family to the corporation.

Since we no longer need our families to buy homes, go to college, or care for us when we are old and incapable of caring for ourselves, we have no real secular need for the family beyond childhood. This means that kids can move across the country or across the world with no financial consequences, and adults have been lifted from the burden of caring for their elderly relatives thanks to retirement accounts managed by the most powerful corporations in the world.

I want Grandma to be taken care of but I think it would be better for her family to do that caring.

I think it is best for people to find the means to purchase their own homes.

The growing distance between family members is a tragedy and nothing less.

Secular reasons for having kids may be selfish, such as seizing opportunities to live through them, possibly saving a bad marriage, and rearing caregivers that will assume responsibility for their elderly parents. The latter, of course, is moot given the shift away from financial dependence on family. I am not advocating for having kids regardless of the reasons—good, bad, or indifferent. Instead, I am acknowledging that secular society has dismissed almost all reasons for having kids, and the nuclear family has suffered as a result. Also, I believe that the stock market and its tools like the 401(k) have played a major role in the death of the family unit.

Perhaps we rely too much on public institutions to keep us on the track toward sainthood when we should remain close to our families and growing our families by raising children despite the financial investment opportunities that exist. The secondary market has played a role in secularizing our society to the point where the family is a distant afterthought behind perceived financial independence. Of course, other factors have contributed to the downfall of the nuclear family; all blame cannot be heaped upon the stock market or even the corrupt financial industry as a whole. The stock market has played a key role—in fact, the key role—in the demise of the family by popularizing retirement accounts, facilitating the growth of tech and other addictive industries, and offering false promises of financial independence.

The family is the primary mechanism for producing saints and bringing glory to God. If we continue to embrace things like the stock market that disconnect families, then we are ignoring our mission here on earth. No matter how difficult it may be, we must go against the grain and fight against things that tear the family apart.

Retirement is an idea that I believe has been a plague on the family and society. The idea that able-bodied people should want to live an easy life and stop working for their fellow man is something that runs very counter to the Christian ideal of loving thy neighbor. If we are able, we should always keep working to help promote the common good. Not too long ago we had pension plans which were, for the most part, an employer saying to an employee that if you work for us, we will take care of you when you are no longer able to work. What began as a righteous premise for attracting top talent, evaporated rather quickly. Over the years, employers began handing over the responsibility of caring for their employees to the ever-growing system of speculation called the stock market. By promoting retirement accounts, the stock market encourages us to set as a goal living an easy life. "Retire early" is a common mantra, but the truth is that investing our hard-earned money in the stock market facilitates inflation, hinders the common good, and divorces compensation from labor.

When we dare to question the legitimacy of stock investing, we are fear-mongered into thinking that if we do not invest in the market, we will not be taken care of in our old age. The last few chapters of this book are dedicated to addressing these fear tactics, offering stock market alternatives that are not alternatives in the true sense, but a complete shift in perspective and goal setting.

OBJECTIONS & RESPONSES

If the idea of the stock market being immoral was broadly accepted, many people would be out of work. Is the market so bad that these people should upend their lives? This would certainly ruin some families.

This exact question is why I stressed early on dealing with difficult ideas and the importance of being gentle with and charitable towards those in a tough situation. Previous chapters go into detail about how bad the stock market actually is. The short answer is that the stock market is that bad, but I do not believe anyone employed in a role inextricably linked to the stock market should make an impulsive or irrational decision about their employment. If you are at least mildly compelled by my arguments, please consider the following.

The stock market has become so ingrained in our society that most who participate in it are unaware of its danger. This means that detaching yourself from the market should probably be done slowly and prudently all while engaging in prayer with our Lord. If you are someone who uses the stock market to support yourself and others, then prayer should be your first step to discerning your next step. Each situation is unique and each relationship with Jesus is unique. For some, like me, the ability to divest and start anew is possible. For others, a slower and more prudent method may need to be the route taken. Yet, there is even another group that may not be able to divest because of extreme circumstances. After all, we are talking about something that is utterly entrenched in our daily lives.

Another pressing question or objection that runs parallel to this objection relates to the financial collapse that would ensue if droves of Christians abruptly abandoned stock trading. If only a small percentage of the supposed 200 million Christians in the U.S. read this book and decide to divest from the market, a major economic collapse might result. A real recession and possibly even a depression would be well underway.

If that many people read this book and are compelled to act because of it, then I missed my calling as a writer. For the sake of argument, let's walk out the potential for this book to go viral, influencing millions to divest. Then certainly a market collapse of some kind could happen. The most concerning chain of events resulting from this sort of financial tsunami is the historic connection between sudden financial devastation and suicide.

Suicide, inability to provide for one's family, and loss of savings are all tragic and I wouldn't want any of these things to happen to anyone. Nevertheless, when sin becomes pervasive and needs to be rooted out, certain difficulties will arise. Most pro-lifers do not give credence to the argument that if you ban abortion, then more mothers will die in shady dark rooms. The reasons this argument is not taken seriously include the fact that statistics prove it wrong, and it is never acceptable to permit a direct evil just to avoid an indirect evil, no matter how tragic. Bad things that indirectly result from truly good actions are not sins that rest on the souls of those committing the good acts. Suicide committed because of financial loss in an illicit market is not the sin of those who decide to abandon the illicit market. To continue the abortion comparison, it is not the fault of those wishing to save the lives of babies that a mother tragically dies in a dark room somewhere trying to kill her baby. There is, however, culpability for the pro-lifer and the market liquidator if they do not share the love of Christ with those on the opposing side when given the chance

Hasn't the market done the opposite of destroying the family by giving the family more financial independence via things like 401(k)s and other retirement accounts?

No, is the quick and easy answer to this objection. The longer answer to this question may seem repetitive, but I will include more depth and details from a different and important angle to drive the point home.

Modern-day finance has shifted individuals' dependence away from the family and towards the financial industry and corporatocracy. The stock market is the primary tool used to accomplish this. This is the reason we have more stuff than we have ever had, but also are in more debt, have children living farther away from their parents in greater numbers, and have fewer people getting married and having children. There is a direct correlation between our increasing reliance on major companies and financial institutions, the value we place on careers with lucrative retirement programs, and the rate at which we devalue the traditional family. We have become blinded by gaining more and more things to increase our levels of comfort, which we mistakenly think will bring us a content heart.

Misguided values have also led to increased suicides, which in the United States spiked 37% between 2000 and 2018.[12] Depression is also on the rise. Major depression is one of the most common mental illnesses, affecting more than 8% (21 million) of American adults each year and 15% of youth ages 12 to 17 (3.7 million).[13] The fact that more people are deciding to not have kids because they would rather pursue careers and material gain, exacerbates the problem. The stock market has played a significant role in the decay of the family and has hurt the whole of Christianity; the two are undeniably linked. Though our Lord is the victor in eternity, at present we are losing souls to the enemy because we have eagerly adopted modern-day financial practices with no regard for what truly matters, namely God and neighbor.

Numerous factors have led to the decay of the family, but dependence shifting from families to financial markets has been detrimental to the fabric of society. Instances of corruption within the financial industry and corporatocracy at large are common. Consider the 2008 financial crash where gold standard financial organizations like Bank of America, Citigroup, J.P. Morgan, Morgan Stanley, State Street Bank, and many others knew they were involved in questionable lending practices but were blinded by the prospect of growing their bottom line. Contrast big

12 Holmes, Leonard. "Suicide Statistics in the United States." Very Well Mind, October 10, 2023, https://www.verywellmind.com/suicide-rates-overstated-in-people-with-depression-2330503. Accessed February 10, 2024.

13 Mental Health America, Depression. "Basic Facts About Depression." MHANational, https://www.mhanational.org/conditions/depression. Accessed January 5, 2024.

banking's appetite for increasing revenue with families' instinctive desire to protect their own at any cost—even in non-Christian families. Of course, some families are terrible, and all fall short of the ideal, but we can acknowledge there is a noble ideal to be had, whereas the model of the financial institution is making profits. Making profits is not a problem in itself; a business is designed for commerce, which is well and good. The problem is in the reliance we now have on the market and the indifference to the family that has resulted.

The question often asked in our society today is, "Why is it that we live in a time of great economic abundance, yet we are becoming more anxious, more depressed, and more suicidal?" The answer is that we have done away with God, family, and neighbor and embraced self and materialism. Can anyone truly deny that buying and selling abstractions has pushed us in this depraved direction?

We used to rely on pension plans that were managed by the places in which we worked, but now we rely on 401(k)s managed by monopolistic financial institutions. We used to rely on family to help purchase a home, but now we rely on loans from predatory lenders. We used to rely on younger generations to take care of older generations, but now we rely on retirement plans and nursing homes even if we have the means to provide and care for our elderly. Each of these shifts has played a role in the decay of the family unit. Like dormant muscles, if we fail to engage with community and family, they will atrophy.

The human person is never completely independent. We have only shifted our dependence from families to institutions and globalist systems like the market. This shift may have made our lives easier in some ways, but certainly not better. Good and easy are not synonymous. All too often they are in opposition.

If you accept this line of reasoning, then you may be tempted to take on a scrupulous critique of other modern-day inventions that have played a role in family decay, like the internet itself. Certainly, an invention dominated by toxic social media use and pornography has played its role in all the previously mentioned societal ills, but it is different in kind than the stock market. The internet, at its core, is just a means of communication. It may be a means of communication that is dominated by spiritually damaging actors, but it remains just a means of communication.

The stock market, on the other hand, is at its core designed to do something immoral in helping people reap where they have not sown and in pushing individuals towards reliance on globalist financial institutions. It can be argued that the internet may need to be radically changed and combatted, or even done away with entirely, but remember that something being used for evil purposes is different from something being inherently evil. A hammer can be used for building a table or committing a murder. The hammer is not inherently evil, but murder is. Conversely, systems like drug cartels and things like Ouija boards are explicitly designed for nefarious purposes.

One more point needs to be made about retirement accounts, which in some ways are the main product of the stock market. Retirement accounts are primarily concerned with laying up treasures here on earth. It is difficult to not think about our Lord's words, "Do not lay up for yourselves treasures on earth... lay up for yourselves treasures in heaven..." (Mt 6:19-20). I am not against preparing for the future, but I do believe our actions should be oriented to our eternal futures instead of illicit activities designed to prepare us for our finite worldly futures. This requires being less focused on ourselves and the nice vacations we'll take when we are older and more focused on building up saints in our families and communities through true labor. The former is not a recipe for promoting the common good, and we should not pursue anything that does not promote the common good.

Many people invest in the market via retirement accounts, and if they accepted this idea of the market being immoral, they would have to pay huge penalties to the government, another immoral institution, to get their money out. Shouldn't they just leave their money where it is?

This objection is really getting to the heart of the matter. If you accept the premise of this book and feel called to take action, you are most likely going to be faced with some difficult choices. Upending your life savings, paying huge fees to the government, and changing your entire thinking in terms of finance are all tough pills to swallow. Yet, they may be necessary if you are going to stick to your moral convictions and promote the common good.

Divesting your retirement account before you are of age can result in major financial penalties where you end up losing 30% of your savings or more. This 30% plus goes directly to local and federal governments, which many people think are just as nefarious as the market itself. It would seem obvious, then, that the solution would be to leave your money in the retirement account and accept the moral loss. However, the case could be made that Uncle Sam is not all bad due to some redeeming qualities like creating infrastructure and reasonable defense measures, while the market is inherently immoral given its design and purpose. Therefore, choosing to give the local and federal authorities money rather than leaving it in the market to do more and more damage over time would be choosing the lesser of two evils.

An additional point could be made that even if the two are equally illicit, taking money out of the stock market, which causes continuous societal bleeding over long time periods, and making a one-time payment to a historically inefficient government would be again choosing the lesser of two evils. While the lesser of two evils is still evil, divesting your interest in the stock market is akin to ripping off a bandage. It hurts but the pain is short-lived. Think about it this way, if you leave all your money in the market, you are contributing 100% to the damage it wreaks upon society.

If you divest and the government penalizes you, your contribution to the ills of society perpetrated by the government involves just 30% of your wealth one time and via a system far less efficient than the market.

The real problem in this objection is that we may lose a good portion of the money we gained, which is emotionally tough to handle given both our obsession with money and our admirable desires to provide for our families. However, just because it is emotionally difficult to part with money that was gained nefariously—knowingly or not—does not mean that it ought not be done.

Again, each situation is completely unique. I personally took the hit of about 30% overall when I divested my retirement account from the NBA, but this may not be the right move for everyone. I had opportunity, time, and profound moral conviction on my side (plus a very impulsive nature). If you are older, you might have the ability to transfer amounts to cash holdings, or you could be legally stuck at no fault of your own.

No matter the situation, if you agree that the stock market is immoral and want to combat it, stop and take time to talk with friends and family, and spend time in prayer with our Lord Jesus Christ before making any major financial decisions. Humans might steer you wrong, but our Lord never will.

PART III

ALTERNATIVES

PREVIEW

At this point, your reaction to my premise may fall in one of three camps: opposition, reluctant agreement, or rapt agreement.

Those in the opposition camp likely find the responses to the objections irksome, yet they sparked enough curiosity to keep you reading. Please be encouraged. Spend time in objective contemplation and discernment, asking our Lord to reveal the truth.

It's likely most readers find themselves in the reluctant agreement camp. The nature and resulting cunning of the stock market amount to disguised evils to which we have been blinded for some time. The realization that the stock market and modern-day investing is not in alignment with Christianity can cause a pitted feeling in the bottom of our stomachs. Realizing something we routinely or passively engage in is causing so much societal strife elicits strong emotions. Even if you agree with the arguments I have laid out, it can be difficult to accept them, making you wish you had simply remained ignorant of the facts. I can relate to this feeling. I wrestled with it for a while, even holding some resentment, for a short while, toward the person who presented these concepts to me.

So, what are we to do? What are the alternatives? Where can we invest? The answers are not easy but they are accompanied by endless possibilities that can be both spiritually and financially fruitful.

As we dive into these alternatives in these final chapters, it is important to understand that you can pursue each of these options with everything you have and still end up completely destitute and unable to provide for yourself someday. I do not believe that will happen, and I have confidence that our Heavenly Father will always provide what we need. Yet, if we do become destitute after trying our best to build up the Kingdom of God by following our Father's will, then so be it! At least our treasure in Heaven will be great. I encourage you to spend some time reflecting on this passage from Luke before diving into this book's stock market alternatives:

> And he said to his disciples, "Therefore I tell you, do not be anxious about your life, what you shall eat, nor about your body, what you shall put on. For life is more than food, and the body more than clothing. Consider the ravens: they neither sow nor reap, they have neither storehouse nor barn, and yet God feeds them. Of how much more value are you than the birds! And which of you by being anxious can add a cubit to his span of life? If then you are not able to do as small a thing as that, why are you anxious about the rest? Consider the lilies, how they grow; they neither toil nor spin; yet I tell you, even Solomon in all his glory was not clothed like one of these. But if God so clothes the grass which is alive in the field today and tomorrow is thrown into the oven, how much more will he clothe you, O men of little faith! And do not seek what you are to eat and what you are to drink, nor be of anxious mind. For all the nations of the world seek these things, and your Father knows that you need them. Instead, seek His kingdom, and these things shall be yours as well. "Fear not, little flock, for it is your Father's good pleasure to give you the kingdom. Sell your possessions and give alms; provide yourselves with purses that do not grow old, with a treasure in the heavens

> that does not fail, where no thief approaches and no moth destroys. For where your treasure is, there will your heart be also (Lk 12:22-34).

To put it plainly, we should ditch the selfish profit motive and direct our focus on Kingdom investing. Matthew 16:25-26 says, "For whoever would save his life will lose it, and whoever loses his life for my sake will find it. For what will it profit a man if he gains the whole world and forfeits his life? Or what shall a man give in return for his life?" This condition of discipleship from Matthew's Gospel sums up our current societal predicament. If we focus on profits, we will lose all that matters, but if we focus on Christ, we will gain all that matters.

One last little caveat that I think will become obvious when exploring these stock market alternatives is that they are not at all one-to-one proportioned alternatives. I oppose buying low and selling high in the stock market because of all the evil that ensues, so if I advocate other investments that entailed buying low, doing no work, and selling high, then the alternatives would be just as evil as the market. Instead, the alternatives I present are mindset changes each of us needs to make. Foremost, each of us will benefit from redefining the word investment. Rather than associating investments with retirement and passive income, let's begin associating investments with building up the Kingdom of God.

CHAPTER 9

RAISING CHRISTIAN FAMILIES

The family is the first and most important alternative investment. The Catechism of the Catholic Church states:

> The family is the cell of social life. It is the natural society in which husband and wife are called to give themselves in love and in the gift of life. Authority, stability, and a *life of relationships* (emphasis added) within the family constitute the foundations for freedom, security, and fraternity within society (2207).

Raising a Christian family is one of the hardest, if not the hardest, things you can attempt in this world. Getting married, having children, staying together, and cultivating a God-fearing and "Jesus, I trust in you" environment is no small feat in a secular world. But with a little grace, it is absolutely possible and has the potential to be far more rewarding than any investment in the stock market.

Sure, raising a Christian family is great and spiritually rewarding, but how is it an alternative to stock market investing which is a financial endeavor?

I once posed this question and expect you might, too. Before modernity consumed us and the world was overtaken by predatory bank loans, inflation-creating retirement accounts, and old people pits (otherwise known as nursing homes … kidding but not really), we relied on, depended on, and sought the help of family. Sure, we have many more things now and many people don't want to be burdened with Grandma taking up an extra seat at the dinner table, but our dependence on institutions over families has given us more economic and spiritual woes than we can count. Not only does our society suffer spiritual ills like anxiety, depression, and suicide as a result of finance-over-family thinking, but we also suffer many financial woes as well. Financial institutions have capitalized on our dependency by getting us into debt and addicted to products all while killing small businesses. All of these factors have hurt the true bottom line of family income. This means that even though we have more things now, we have less financial independence. Broadly speaking, people today can obtain an iPhone but are less connected to family and are heavily reliant on a finance industry that views them only as a bank account.

True wealth is spiritual in nature and comes from us emptying ourselves of things so that Jesus can fill us up with Himself. A perfect way to do this is to focus on the family and the uber-crucial role Christ plays in the family. What better way to learn to be a servant like Christ the King than to care for our children and elderly parents? However, wealth, in the purely financial sense, is deserving of some of our attention as well, and it is, I believe, of great importance that we rethink what it means to be financially wealthy. Currently, most think of financial wealth as being able to do what you want and obtain what you want because of a healthy bank account. As Christians, we should challenge this secular notion by proposing a new one. Namely, financial wealth should involve relying on family over corporations and striving to provide the necessities for a saintly life. The reason both my proposed definition of financial wealth and the standard definition have an aspect of dependence is that no matter what we do, we will always be dependent on someone or something. The question is to whom or what should we give our dependence? Family or corporation?

Now let us be honest, such a Christ-centered, family-over-finance approach could lead initially to indigence but it will be short-lived. You may have more spiritual fruit in your life, but if that is not enough of a motivator, then think about the long-term prospects for your family and future generations. Not only will they be better off spiritually, but they also will be less connected to monopolistic corporations, predatory banks, and illicit markets.

It is not lost on me how difficult it is to put into practice alternatives to secular investing. The challenge of focusing on the spiritual rather than the temporal seems to defy our natural survival instincts, not to mention it is inconvenient and uncomfortable, but let's ask ourselves a few questions. Should we physically care for our sick and elderly, or should we disconnect them from our family and push their problems onto someone else? Should we participate in our company's 401(k) because it's lucrative and easy, or should we seek the harder, less traveled path that results in a deeper family connection? Should we promote and incentivize predatory lending by banks to buy a home just so we can have some freedom from our families, or should we learn how to build up our families without reliance on corrupt financial institutions?

The point is that the true Christian family is the answer to many modern-day evils. We rely on the stock market because we want to retire safely and enjoy our golden years without worrying about familial responsibilities, but this is simply not what we are called to by Christ. This life has many joys, but our aspiration should not and cannot be slothfulness! If we change our fixation from easy retirement to building up a devout Christian family, then our futures will take care of themselves, especially our eternal ones. And this is the point I really want to drive home. When we hear the word invest, we need to stop thinking about retirement and start thinking about the beatific vision.

I want to make it clear that it is not wrong or sinful to save for the future, in fact, that is the responsible thing to do; however, being consumed with saving for the future to the point that we lose sight of the eternal and engage willingly or not in financial corruption is extremely detrimental to society and to ourselves.

It is important to realize that everyone has a role to play in building up Christian families. This message is not meant for just parents but is intended for all members of the family. Adult children, single aunts and uncles, and grandparents are all needed if we are going to build up truly connected Christian families. It is a community effort. The entire family needs to readjust their thinking, refocus themselves on the will of God, and move away from the will of BlackRock. This looks like brothers helping brothers obtain housing for their families, sisters helping sisters care for their young, grandparents helping raise the children and in return being cared for by the children. All these things are needed if we are to shift our reliance away from the finance industry and back to the family.

The most beautiful part of the refocus on the family as a true investment is that it will hopefully help all members grow in their relationship with Jesus and with each other, but another great potential result is the economic success it can create. When families rely on each other, it typically creates a scenario where many people are working towards a common goal out of love. This means these families are less likely to be in debt, more likely to achieve business success, and more motivated to achieve goals because the motivating factor is familial love. This sentiment may seem anecdotal, but research shows the most successful family units, families that stay together and have adequate economic means, are those who sacrifice modern-day comforts for the good of one another. This does not mean that financial gain is guaranteed. I am not a fan of the prosperity gospel, but God typically provides what is needed when we follow His will. Below is a brief example of how true financial wealth can be obtained through a Jesus and family-first way of thinking.

> A young couple gets married. We'll call them Joe and Sally Smith. Joe and Sally work average-paying jobs. In some time, they have their first child and can afford a fixer-upper house with the help of a bank loan. Their extended family either does not have the means to help or they disagree with the concepts in this book. The Smiths end up having five children, and though they can put food on the table because they are frugal, they probably won't be able to put each child through college or afford extravagant weddings for their daughters.
>
> Joe and Sally do a great job sharing the gospel and the love of Christ with their kids. Only time will tell if each child keeps the faith or falls away.
>
> When the Smiths approach retirement age, both agree that Sally should retire first because of health conditions, and that Joe, who is in good health, will continue working for the sake of the family and his Christian moral convictions.
>
> At the end of their lives, they do not have much, but their little house is paid for and they have modest savings. The Smiths have not gone on fancy vacations or driven nice cars, but they cultivated a loving home and now they can leave a little something to their kids.
>
> One kid buys out his other siblings and gets the house at a discount because his siblings were taught charity by their loving parents. The sibling who gets the house has a jumpstart on life because he is not as indebted to a bank as his parents were, and he can be of more assistance to his other siblings as they start their families.
>
> Each of the Smiths' children is wise, heeds the Word of Christ, and follows their parents' example, choosing to be

> frugal, build up little nest eggs, pay off their homes, and leave their kids with a better starting point than they had.
>
> Homes and small nest eggs are then left to kids of future generations, and soon loans from banks are not entirely needed by descendants of the Smith family. Retirement accounts are the last thing on their minds because each has been raised to know that family is there for them and that they are there for the others.
>
> By not investing in the market, this family's financial progress may be a little slower, but their reliance on each other has enabled them to start businesses, free themselves of debt, and most importantly create a Christ-centered family that is growing, connected, and willing to care for one another for the long-term. They have built true generational wealth.

The Smiths' example may seem like an impossible pie-in-the-sky idea because life and outside influences could get in the way, tragedy could strike, some members of the family might stray from the faith, move away to pursue careers, or marry poorly. It is important to remember, however, that just because the ideal is difficult and unlikely does not mean we should not pursue it. It is precisely because of a lack of pursuit that such ideals are rarely realized.

I am not suggesting that four generations of one family should squeeze into a 900-square foot home to save money. Healthy boundaries need to be set. I am advocating for families supporting one another in times of need and in financial endeavors, and appropriately sharing financial successes all for the glory of God.

CHAPTER 10

BUILDING CHRISTIAN COMMUNITIES

Building a Christian community, much like raising a Christian family, is a difficult accomplishment, but it is possible and absolutely needed! To combat the ills of this world, especially financial ones, thriving and deeply rooted Christian communities are a must. God, through His grace and perfect wisdom, allows us to participate in such spiritual battles because this type of work not only combats evil, but also strengthens our faith. What better investment could you make in your true future than doing something that combats evil and strengthens your faith?

Building Christian communities does not require leaving civilized society to start a commune somewhere. I have nothing against secluded religious life, the Lord knows we need the prayers of those that choose such a lifestyle. We also can learn a lot from monks, friars and nuns regarding what true community looks like. The point of focus here is that the Gospel calls us to evangelize to the ends of the earth, and hiding away from the rest of the world does not sound too evangelistic. Rather, take initiative to make sure your local church/parish is thriving and that the people in the community know that the local church and the local Christians are there for those in need. Youth groups, young adult groups, grief groups, food pantries, Bible studies, pilgrimages, potlucks, sports leagues, Theology on Tap talks, and everything else the Christian mind can think of needs to be thriving. The secular world is all too eager to pick up our slack if our faith practice is lacking. If we do not offer these resources to our communities, then someone else will offer a spiritually perverted and financially depraved alternative.

When the local Church and the local Christians fail to provide financial relief to those in need, we get predatory lenders, impotent and costly government-sponsored welfare, and a desperate populace. Likewise, when the Christian community fails to provide or at least be involved in sports leagues and offer youth programs, we get money-hungry and idolatry-promoting AAU (Amateur Athletic Union) programs and social media-addicted kids. The secular culture will always have a leg up on Christian culture when it comes to alluring the masses because it caters to our natural disposition of pursuing the pleasures of the flesh, but this can be fought against if we simply speak out, evangelize, and offer a quality-driven alternative. Words without action will pave, and have paved, the way for secular culture.

Offering an alternative to the secular culture by building up Christian communities is one of the best spiritual and financial investments we can make. The spiritual benefits are easily discerned, but it can be a bit tougher to understand the potential financial benefits that community-building can bring. How can introducing quality competition to secular culture by offering things like prayer-filled neighborhood potlucks, gospel-focused youth groups, and well-done Christian-led community events result in personal financial gain? Before I answer that difficult question directly, consider the progression of Christian community-building efforts:

1. Begin Christian community-building through events, groups, and other endeavors.
2. View these opportunities as platforms for sharing the gospel.
3. SHARE THE GOSPEL. (Mission accomplished! We could end here, but let's keep going.)

4. Realize an increase in participation, thanks to newly evangelized individuals. Truth inspires!
5. Benefit from increased resources, resulting from increased participation. It's a positive domino effect.
6. Reach more who are in need. This may require creating a Christian-based council or community credit union for proper distribution of funds. Something as simple as a checks and balances agreement with the parish finance council can suffice.
7. Rely less on secular institutions because the community has developed a sound means of local support.
8. Enjoy a prevailing Christian culture because there is little need for or reliance on secular institutions.
9. Promote the common good. A more prevalent Christian culture lifts everyone!

When this concept was first presented to me, I had two initial concerns. Perhaps you can relate. First, cajoling family and neighbors sounds like impossible work. Second, how would such a community endeavor translate to financial stability for me or any individual?

The first point is easily addressed. Yes, it is going to be arduous work, but that's one of the beautiful things about our Lord Jesus Christ. With Him, nothing is impossible. As I stated previously, even if the ideal is hard, it should still be pursued.

Two obstacles make individual financial flourishing particularly challenging: obscurity and temptation. We should not build Christian communities or even raise Christian families if our only motivation is to one day fill our own pockets. This is the temptation every Christian church, business, and non-profit faces. Are we doing this whole Christian thing because it will beef up our bank accounts or do we believe in the Gospel? This is a struggle I personally deal with constantly. This struggle is only overcome through time with our Lord and constantly checking our motivations in a truly honest way.

Another difficulty regarding community building and financial success relates to indirect and hidden means. When we invest time, labor, and capital to build Christian culture in our communities, we are likely not going to see a direct positive effect in our monthly income, but we will find more friendships, a sense of belonging, and a deeper, more persevering faith. These positive outcomes from building Christian communities will lead to a healthier mindset, better personal decision-making, and trust that our communities have our back. All these things are essential for excelling in economics and life in general. Yes, the financial success realized as a result of investing in building Christian communities may be completely indirect and unobvious, but it is still present. Just because we do not see an extra comma in our bank accounts immediately after making an effort in our communities does not mean we will never reap financial gain from Christian community-building.

At the end of your life, will you prefer loving families and Christ-centered communities or a healthy bank account? I know we would all prefer both, and achieving both is possible with some hard work and a lot of grace. However, all too often chasing dollars results in familial and spiritual ruin. On the other hand, when we chase relationships centered on Christ, blessings, one way or another, are inevitable. Simply stated, I find it hard to believe that our Lord would not give us our "daily bread" if we spend our time trying to build up the Kingdom of God.

Both the community and family building alternatives to the stock market require a lot of work, and the personal financial payoffs are either indirect or potentially non-existent, but they are the Christian ideal and should be pursued. Plus, they have the purpose and potential to truly provide for us in possible times of need. A healthy bank account certainly has its benefits, but ill-gotten gains will always be spiritually destructive. While on the other hand, Christ-centered relationships with our families, friends, and communities will provide us with what we truly need and desire.

The final point I want to emphasize with regards to community and family building is the idea of proximity. Proximity could be considered the lynchpin of these alternatives to the stock market. In order for us to raise Christian families and build Christian communities, we need to live close to family and close to our desired communities. The Devil has taught us to pursue well-paying jobs and retirement accounts with no concern for moving away from our families and communities, and this has caused generations of people to be isolated and miserable. Think of how common it is for the child to move across the country to obtain a "good" job without giving their family a second thought. Sure, in today's world, we have Facetime and cross-country flights that give us the illusion of connectivity, but there is something important about physically being with one another on a regular basis. This is why none of the sacraments of the Catholic Church can be administered remotely or by phone. If we are going to raise Christian families and keep our families Christian, then we must, at the very least, live near our families. If we are going to build Christian communities, then we need to be present in those communities.

Before my personal conversion, I picked up and moved away from my parents, sister, and grandparents, without a second thought, to be with my future wife and in an area that could pay me a higher salary. I don't necessarily regret this move because it played a role in my conversion and ultimately brought me to our Lord Jesus Christ, but it obviously put a strain on my family and stagnated familial relationships that otherwise could have flourished. Genesis 2:24 says a man is to leave his parents and cling to his wife, but that verse refers to the man's responsibility to forgo dependency on parents and embark on the mission of caring for his wife. It is not about dismissing his parents altogether and leaving them. We know this because the fourth commandment instructs children to honor thy mother and father.

If we stay physically present with our families and communities, they will thrive, and probably thrive financially. Being close to one another means we can lighten each other's loads and give spiritual and financial relief to one another. The money saved on childcare alone is astronomical if we just have family close by. I guarantee it will take you just a few minutes of contemplation to understand how beneficial all aspects of life could be if we have Christ-centered loved ones close by.

IMPORTANT SIDENOTE

Some family members may be detrimental to the physical, mental, and spiritual wellbeing of you and your immediate family. Pray for these individuals, reaching out to them only when appropriate without forcing ourselves upon them. Christ never forces someone into believing in Him and we should not either. If a parent or sibling does not want to be a part of your Christian family and community building, then so be it. Pray for them and live by example as best you can.

CHAPTER 11

STARTING CHRISTIAN BUSINESSES

Raising Christian families and building Christian communities are the most important alternatives to the stock market, but their financial benefits can be indirect and tough to wrap our secularized minds around. This is not the case with the alternatives presented in this and the next two chapters because these are more economic in nature.

Creating and participating in Christian business is one of the best ways to secure your financial future without sacrificing your eternal future. Starting a business and creating a product or service that people need is always going to be a surefire way to obtain financial wealth. Proof of this can be found when looking at a list of the richest people in the world. Elon Musk and Jeff Bezos are, at the time of this writing, numbers two and three on the list of the world's richest people. The reason they are both on this list is that they created a product (Tesla) and a service (Amazon), respectively, that satisfied the wants and needs of the masses, and they were compensated as no other human beings have ever been compensated. While Amazon and Tesla may not be conducting themselves with Christian values in mind, they are excellent examples of how true fortunes are amassed by creating and producing something of value.

Let's apply that principle to Christian business. A Christian business is not necessarily one like a Christian bookstore that screams "Jesus Christ is King" at every turn, though there is nothing wrong with that. A Christian business can be a local auto body shop, barber, pizza place, car wash, accountant, law firm, or anything that works toward the common good and conducts itself in accordance with Christian values. A Christian business is simply a business that refuses to cave to sin. If you're running a profitable pizza shop, then donate some of your food to underprivileged schools; if you operate an auto body shop, then charge reasonable and transparent prices; if you're the local barber, then sponsor a backpack drive. Simply conducting business honorably without pursuing the almighty dollar at any cost is the makings of a Christian business.

A Christian business should simply be recognizable to customers as a Christian business. This does not mean that you have to have crucifixes all over your pizza shop or pray with everyone who sits in your barber chair (though there's nothing wrong with these things). It means people receive a little bit of the light of Christ when they interact with your business. This can be because of little things like charging fair prices, greeting customers with kindness, or not tolerating profane or illicit behavior in your business.

Now that we have an idea of what a Christian business is, let's talk about some of the struggles associated with launching a business, especially a Christ-centered business. Starting a business is risky, no question about it. Startups can easily lead to financial disaster. On top of financial risks, there are emotional and spiritual risks. From attracting and serving customers, to managing employees, products and services, government regulations, and bookkeeping, it is easy to get bogged down and stressed out with all you have to do to keep the business thriving. The worst part of running your own business is probably various forms of temptation. You can be tempted to "cook the books" or make some illicit compromises in your operations just to turn a greater profit. You may also be tempted to be a harsh employer because of stress or because of past experiences that have left you jaded. Are you motivated to go start a business yet?

Starting and running a business is difficult and comes with many pitfalls. I find, however, that business owners who make it beyond the startup phase are typically the most financially well-off people on the planet. Running a business comes with a lot of work, a lot of headaches, and a lot of risks, but the reward potential is extraordinarily high because of the freedom and potential for the good it provides. The inevitable failures suffered from starting your own business and the resilient perseverance that results from those failures are great for the soul and can lead to a level of self-sufficiency that most of humanity misses. Think about the most successful person you know, in terms of finances, who is also great at getting things done. Chances are this person, in one way or another, runs their own business. My consensus is obvious to most, and many books have been written about entrepreneurship and how financially lucrative and rewarding it can be. I recommend these books on the subject, though I do not fully endorse everything found within their pages: *Zero to One* by Peter Thiel, *Start with Why* by Simon Sinek, and *Rich Dad Poor Dad* by Robert Kiyosaki.

Allow me to also highlight the freedom associated with running a business. The freedom that comes with being a business owner increases the financial risk and reward exponentially, but it also leads to a similar spiritual dynamic. The freedom to be in complete control of a profitable business comes with a choice. To whom should the control be given? You? A board of directors? Some consultant? Your kids? Or God? If God is given control, then blessings are inevitable in one way or another! Yet, if control is kept from God and reserved for you or another, then financial blessings may come, but spiritual fruit will not be present. When you have much, choosing to give it up or keep it, whether spiritually or economically, has great consequences.

Starting a Christian business is not the only portion of this alternative. The second part is participating in Christian business, which comes with fewer headaches. I understand that it is not in the cards for everyone to start their own business and run it successfully; some are needed to work for such businesses to help them flourish. Working for a Christian business is just as important as starting a Christian business.

Participating in Christian business is a call to action. If you are working for an employer right now who is asking you to do some sinful or sketchy things, then try to enact change or leave that job. Go out and find a business that is, at the very least, tolerant of your Christianity, or maybe even find one that is promoting Christian virtue. Of course, potentially leaving a job should involve a great deal of prayer, contemplation and conversations with family and friends. If your job requires participation in questionable activities or serving untoward clients and you stay for security's sake, then the question of "Jesus, do I trust you?" must be asked honestly.

"Jesus, I trust in you" is a prayer that we need to live out every day, especially as business owners and participants. The Devil uses jobs and false security to keep us imprisoned in sin and beholden to a corrupt global economic matrix. If we truly want to break free, then we must trust in Jesus and take appropriate risks for the betterment of the Kingdom. Starting Christian businesses, working for Christian employers, or enacting change in our current work environment is what we all must do if we want to combat the hold that the Devil has on us, our families, and our communities. The task is not an easy one, but it is one worth doing for the sake of our emotional, spiritual, and financial health.

Participating in a Christian business may be easier than starting and running a Christian business, but like all stock market alternatives, it involves a fair amount of work. If we are able, we are called by our Lord to labor, and this is for good reason. This book's alternatives are primarily focused on investing for the eternal future because, as the great Christian apologist C.S.

Lewis once wrote, "Aim at heaven and you will get earth thrown in. Aim at earth and you get neither." This quote is not meant to point us in the direction of the prosperity gospel. Instead, it affirms Jesus' call to seek first His kingdom and appreciation and gratitude for the joys of this life will be ours.

The secular goal of an early retirement where we can do what we want when we want, made possible by a nefarious system like the stock market, is simply not putting us on the straight and narrow path. There is too much "we," "I," and moral depravity in these goals and not enough Jesus. Modern-day financial goals continuously push us towards a nihilistic materialism, causing us to covet an easy and secure old age, which we may never see, at the expense of true spiritual fruit. This is why the alternatives to the stock market require labor. The alternatives must be different in kind than what we are currently doing, because both our goals and the means by which we seek to achieve them are missing the mark.

CHAPTER 12

OWNING PROPERTY

Owning property is one of the truly time-tested ways to build wealth and provide for your family. More books have been written and talks given on this subject than could be consumed in a lifetime. Let's focus on traits that make up the Christian property owner, namely integrity, honesty, respect, and a sense of duty. A Christian property owner should not have the sole intention of making a profit. Rather, the primary focus of the Christian property owner should be to provide affordable and quality housing to people who need it. Christian property owners should care for the possessions that have been entrusted to them by God. Fix caved-in floors, broken locks, and busted windows, and don't overcharge for rent just because you can. Basically, don't be a slumlord; be a Christian!

Even if you're not renting out properties, and the only living space you own is your own, take care of it. Don't be slothful and let it decay. Make sure it is maintained so the next person, who may be one of your children, can live in it and thrive. Of course, you don't have to have all the latest bells and whistles in your home, and if you are decorating a room to which toddlers or young children have access, then you'll want to be especially economical because destruction is inevitable in that room. Make all upgrades and repairs that ought to be done and do them within reason.

The wily real estate market makes obtaining investment properties challenging. Sky-high prices prove my point about inflation and my soon-to-be-made point about predatory lending.

So, how do we obtain one of the best possible investment assets if we can't afford it? The answer is one of the many reasons why raising Christian families should be priority number one in moral investing. You may not be able to afford a home by yourself, but with enough work, cooperation, and grace, your family might. Maybe you and some siblings or parents can invest in property together. Maybe your kids can come together and purchase a property as a unit.

I realize buying and owning a home with family may sound awful for more reasons than you can list. Hard work, cooperating with and listening to each other, mingling finances, and making decisions via committee is arduous. Yet it may be necessary for the sake of investing in a licit manner. Also, keep in mind that though it is ideal for all parties involved to be convicted by Christian morality and social teaching, collective owning of property can still be done ethically with predominantly secular families. Some cultures, such as Romanians and various groups of Indians have had great financial success and kept their families intact for generations by practicing collective owning of property among the broader family.

The financial industry and the government are set up, whether intentionally or by accident, to keep us separated from our families. I believe it is a carefully orchestrated plot by Satan himself. Welfare, subsidy checks, and child tax credits keep us attached to the government and disconnected from family. IRAs, 401(k)s, mutual funds, and bank lending practices keep us reliant on institutions instead of on family. We may naturally look at working with our family as a ridiculous idea fraught with potential for feuding and be more at ease with investing with faceless entities in government and industry, even though we complain about those institutions every chance we get. Now is as good a time as any to put our money and our labor where our mouth is.

Please note that although I express disdain for government programs that make us reliant in a direct financial way on the government, I do not have total disdain for all government agencies and programs. I am not advocating for anarchy, but for ordered liberty. I appreciate and respect our police, firefighters, public utilities, etc. If not for the men and women serving the common good in these capacities, we would not have a society, much less one working collectively towards the common good.

Well-meaning programs like state-sponsored welfare and child tax credits incentivize single motherhood and having children for the wrong reasons. A police force, on the other hand, is necessary because we live in a fallen world and need protection from people who mean to do our families and us physical harm.

Also, please know that by suggesting we put our money where our mouth is and start working on community building and raising up families, I am not condemning those who do not quit their jobs and give all their money and time to community efforts. I realize not everyone can do that. The point is to be prudent. If you are convinced by the arguments in this book, begin putting them into action.

I was blessed beyond measure to be able to quit my job, divest of my abstract assets, and land a job with my local Catholic parish and Catholic school. I make a lot less money but am grateful for the opportunities I have, including the ability to launch a website dedicated to promoting the ideals expressed in this book. Because of my age and my extremely supportive family, I was able to leverage my talent and follow my convictions. These conditions were a gift. Each of us needs to find our unique gifts and leverage them to build the Kingdom. It could be as simple as volunteering at church one day a week or mentoring someone. We should remain mindful that each person's situation is unique.

A COMMON REAL ESTATE INVESTMENT HURDLE

Over-extending ourselves is a tangible possibility in Christian property investing. It's not uncommon to purchase a rental property with the intention of fixing it up but never getting around to it because of life's demands. What then? What should we do? If we sell it for a profit simply because the housing market is up, wouldn't we be reaping where we have not sown? Yet wouldn't it be imprudent if we sell it only for what we paid? Owning property is categorically different from owning an abstraction like stocks and ETFs. Purchasing a home requires mounds of paperwork, loan approval from a lender or family member, demonstration of fiscal responsibility, and responsibility for property maintenance, for tax payments, and in some cases for injuries incurred on the property. Selling the property involves getting it into top condition to show it, marketing it, and completing more paperwork. Even if you didn't get to redo the kitchen, you still assumed responsibility for a tangible asset, which is true ownership, unlike the false ownership of shareholding.

Owning property presents the possibility of performing true labor, whereas stock ownership does not. Even though you should attempt to improve the home in some way by the sweat of your brow before selling it, it is morally acceptable to sell a home at fair market value without doing major renovations, as long as this was not the intent at the outset. I am not encouraging slum lording. If you or anyone you know has purchased both a home and a stock, could you say each process entailed the same amount of work and labor? My homebuying experience was a much more labor-intensive and community-based process than when I used to buy stocks and ETFs on my smartphone.

Tangible > *Abstraction* should be a motto we all embrace.

To drive home the point, consider the following. If you buy a home and sit on it for 30 years without doing a thing to it, much like we do with our 401(k)s, do you really think that the house would sell for more than the purchasing price, adjusted for inflation? Of course not. The grass would be overgrown, the roof would be dilapidated, pipes may have burst, the heating and cooling system would be worthless, and countless other problems would have arisen that would make the house plummet in value, making it almost impossible and maybe even illegal to sell.

REAL ESTATE INVESTMENT TRUSTS

A final point regarding real estate investments has to do with Real Estate Investment Trusts (REIT). Most consider REITs more favorable to stocks and ETFs in terms of financial security and moral uprightness. I will leave the financial security aspect up to the analysts, but the moral case is weak. Some will say that REITs are morally preferable to stocks because REITs help create and maintain brick-and-mortar buildings and do not support corrupt corporations. This may be the case, but it is a non-starter because REITs still fall into the reaping-where-one-has-not-sown category. When you invest in a REIT, you are doing no real labor and expecting to be rewarded for it. Even if the REIT helps create an apartment complex or building that promotes the common good, it would not be morally permissible because you are being compensated for doing nothing except handing over money. My arguments against stocks apply also to REITs.

The idea of stored labor is a frequent rebuttal to my arguments. Please refer to Chapter 7, Greed, Sloth, and Other Vices, and specifically to my response to the final objection regarding the nature of currency in modern society. In detail, I explain why compensation should not be divorced from true labor. Just because we performed productive work in the past does not mean we should receive compensation in the present or future that is divorced from that labor. Working a career in some meaningful field and then using the money earned to invest in abstractions does not magically make investing in abstractions morally just. Former righteousness is not a pass for future sin.

CHAPTER 13

CURRENCY REPLACEMENT

Bitcoin (BTC), Ethereum (ETH), gold, silver, and other cryptos and metallics are considered by many to be possible replacements for government-backed fiat currency. I personally am no fan of the current fiat currency, but I am not particularly convinced that a certain crypto or metallic would be a great replacement. Rather, I am not convinced that they could be made into a viable replacement. However, if you think gold or Bitcoin should become the basis of money, then a potentially licit "investment" opportunity arises.

Let's imagine you are buying BTC so that you can make a profit when it goes up in value. Then you are once again going against the premise of this book. If we buy gold only to store it in our basement and sell it when it becomes financially advantageous, then we are expecting a return for doing nothing. Buying gold cannot be compared to my earlier example of buying a home and not renovating it in some way because buying and selling gold requires a few clicks on the internet or a phone call. No one who lives in reality would think purchasing gold is comparable to buying and owning property.

Some, however, view buying a metallic as morally just compared to crypto because metallics are a natural resource, while crypto is an internet abstraction. I too favor the tangible over the abstract, especially when it comes to economics. Nevertheless, an argument for either crypto or a metallic only carries weight if you think they can be a good replacement for the current currency.

Both gold and BTC fall into the trap of speculation if they are not utilized in some real way.

Many people buy cryptos with no intention of ever using them as currency. Instead, cryptos are broadly used as an investable asset that is to be bought low and sold high. This is why the major cryptos of today move in sync with run-of-the-mill tech stocks.

This speculative treatment of crypto has also been a huge cause of its volatility. The collapse of many crypto-based businesses has been at least partially caused by the speculative treatment of crypto. The collapse of FTX, a once major crypto exchange, is just one prime example (though many factors contributed to the FTX implosion). Of course, anything as new as cryptos will experience a great deal of volatility, but the speculative treatment cryptos receive has only compounded and prolonged the volatility issue. If crypto enthusiasts truly want to replace a government fiat currency, then they should use crypto as currency any and every chance they get, while being a vocal activist for crypto as a form of money. If this advocacy is not done and an investor just sits on his crypto waiting for a chance to sell, then the investment is immoral, and the investor is perpetuating the problems that plague cryptocurrencies and our society.

This sentiment of promoting crypto as a real currency goes for metallics as well. If one were to invest in metals, that investment only becomes morally permissible if the purchaser becomes an advocate for putting us back on the gold standard. If the gold is just left to collect dust in your home until a later date when it can bring in a hefty profit, then the investment becomes immoral. Labor is always required to make an investment moral.

I currently do not own metallics or crypto for a few reasons. The first reason is I do not have confidence in myself to stay true to the moral mandate of being a boisterous advocate for fiat replacement. Another reason I do not own metallics or crypto is that I am not yet convinced of their ability to adequately replace fiat currency, of which I am not a fan. Still, the ultimate reason I do not own either asset is that I am skeptical of having such widespread currency in the first place, especially in the case of crypto.

Let's unpack my reservation about metallics and crypto in light of my admitted issues with fiat currency. I do not think either asset is a great replacement for fiat currency like the U.S. dollar because both assets have unique and glaring problems. Fiat currency also has issues, but when selecting a currency for a global state of affairs, we inevitably choose the lesser evil.

Gold has already been tested and failed because the gold standard is a façade. Powerful governments are able to dictate the price of gold, thus treating it like fiat currency. BTC, the king of crypto, seems to not be as decentralized as originally thought since the big players, commonly called whales, are able to manipulate it with ease for their own financial gain. Also, one of BTC's biggest positive claims is that it is finite, but since it can be infinitely divided into the smallest of fractions, the BTC cap is meaningless. Some may buy and store metals and cryptos as an insurance policy, and I would never condemn anyone for doing this, but I believe the point is being missed. If the world goes to hell in a hand basket, the things that will be of value are food, shelter, water, fire power and people, not useless shiny metals or abstract cryptos. The real problem we face is the globalized and dependent economy, and no form of currency will fix this problem. The solution to this problem is Sainthood and building up that Christian culture at a local level.

I am skeptical about widespread monetary systems, which is another reason I do not favor owning things like BTC, ETH, and metals. I am no fan of globalism, and I think that a globalist or even just a very large geographic economy will inevitably lead to secularism and isolation. The only idea that I would ever be willing to promote globally is that of authentic Christianity. The only entity that I can think of that could have the power and will to promote a worldwide currency is the World Economic Forum (WEF), but WEF leaders appear to be completely opposed to Christian values in just about every conceivable way. Therefore, the best way to enact the cultural changes proposed in this book is to implement them at the local level. Given our current state of affairs, any talk about changing the national or global currency would be akin to piloting a spaceship before we could even crawl.

Please do not let my currency pessimism dissuade you from trying to inspire the change in which you believe. I may be wrong about the potential for a currency replacement, and some crypto or natural resource could be the perfect fit; the movement just needs a few virtuous and outspoken people to set it in motion. My point is that simply buying crypto, metallics, or anything else as a speculative investment is morally sketchy. If you are going to invest in these things, then promote their actual utility. If you are part of the effort that leads to them replacing fiat currencies, then you may become wealthy one day.

BONUS SECTION

CHAPTER 14

USURY IS STILL A SIN

Is lending at reasonable rates of interest wrong? What do reasonable rates of interest mean? The Church is against usury, but it seems to be okay with lending at interest, right? What is the difference between usury and lending?

These are difficult questions and have been tackled by many people much more qualified than I. In the debate on usury, some compare teachings of St. Thomas Aquinas to those of Pope St. John Paul II, or a Psalm against a Gospel verse. The confusion stems from the idea that money was once a barren asset that could not be used to produce, and now it is not a barren asset and can be used to produce. It was once like bread that needed to be consumed, but now it is like a hammer and can be used to make things, primarily more money.

Those who say that all interest charging is wrong tend to use arguments from Saint Thomas and others who were not privy to money's transformation. Those who adopt modern ideas about accepting interest use recent church teachings, correctly or incorrectly, and the progress of today's financial systems to support their claims. I wrestled with this argument myself for a long time and have come to a both/and conclusion.

The nature of money has changed, as I discussed earlier in this book. I also stated, however, that this change is probably not for the best. This has led me to conclude that we need to drastically alter how we think of lending with interest. Let's dig a little deeper into this topic.

First, because inflation is predominantly out of the individual's control, we should allow for interest-taking at rates of inflation. Anything beyond the rate of inflation would seem to produce a reaping-where-you-have-not-sown problem, which goes against moral Christian investing, and the premise of this book. Conversely, taking an interest rate that is equal to the rate of inflation would equate to getting back what you lent.

I understand that modern-day lenders do a lot of work to find qualified borrowers and to mitigate risk, but is this work being done to promote the common good? Lending at interest has encouraged many to lend, allowed others to start businesses, and allowed our economy to flourish in some ways. Despite the good that results from starting a productive business, however, it seems that lending money solely to acquire more money in return and without producing anything, has the same negative societal effects as investing in the stock market. Many, if not all, of the arguments I have made against the stock market can be applied to this lending-at-interest concept.

Of course, in the best scenario, lending money enables another to do productive work that promotes the common good, but that does not mean the lender has done productive work. There are two common objections to this:

1. IT IS NECESSARY – People often claim that if we stopped lending money at interest, then no one would lend, and many people would be unable to start businesses or buy homes and cars.
2. IT IS WORK – People also claim lending should be considered productive work for the common good because so much gets done as a result of it.

The first objection regarding the necessity of lending at interest is just admitting that we are flawed and uncharitable and not even willing to attempt to be better. If charity is the principal virtue of Christianity, then could anyone deny that it would be better to give without demanding more in return than it is to give and demand interest? If we lend, then we are naturally giving from our abundance, and are we not called to give from our abundance freely? The resources and materials to build homes, cars, and businesses are always there because they exist in God's creation. The only reason they are unobtainable for some without usurious practices is that inflation and greed have run rampant and made these things too expensive. If our solution to this problem is to keep the systems in place that have caused the problems, then the problems will persist.

Consider this: If lending at interest is so great and allows us to do so much, why are homes, cars, and college educations becoming less and less affordable as we continue to advance in this current economic system?

I bought a home in the middle of the Covid-19 pandemic for the list price of $136,000, and I got a favorable interest rate. This was before I had moral convictions about the stock market or usury. If I stick to the proposed 30-year payoff plan, I will have paid almost $300K for my home, more than double the list price. Neither the home builder, the real estate agent, nor the appraiser is making the most money off the purchase of the home; the lender is. Not those who labored to find a buyer, built a shelter for a family, or even the person who made sure the home was safe, but the person who just gave from their abundance is the one who reaps the greatest reward. Some may argue that the lenders took the greatest risk, but did they? Laws in our country will reward the lenders if I default on my mortgage. The lenders can garnish my wages or even repossess my home. If they repossess my home, then they acquire an asset that, over time, usually appreciates. Does this sound like risky behavior to you?

We must find it in ourselves to be charitable and, if necessary, become financial martyrs so that future generations can free themselves from financial dependence on corrupt corporations that make up a corrupt system. Putting it simply, we ought to give freely, and if lending stops because no one is willing to give freely, then a hard look in the mirror and some time with our Lord should be our medicine.

To be clear, I am not opposed to lending outright. I think it is permissible to take interest at the rate of inflation, collect late fees for delayed back payment, and recover the money you loaned if you need it. What I oppose and think all Christians should oppose is loaning money and collecting more money in return without doing productive labor.

The second objection carries a little more weight. Lending at interest seems, at the very least, to have helped produce a lot of good. Yet, we know that flawed means do not justify good ends. A home purchased for a young family (which is a good thing), thanks to lending at interest, does not justify lending at interest if the practice promotes greed, family decay, unnecessary inflation, and other societal ills.

Perhaps you find yourself convinced that the stock market may produce these ills, but you do not see the connection with lending at interest. This is understandable given the fact that lending requires a bit more work in the secular sense. Finding borrowers and mitigating risk are difficult things, but they are things that are done from a selfish point of view. The lenders who demand arbitrary interest are not lending so that a family can purchase a home, or a business can be started; they are lending to line their own pockets. If they were lending out of charity, then interest would not be demanded and vetting the borrower might not be as intense since the borrower would not have to pay back exceedingly more than what was lent.

Oh, but what if they know they could lend to more people and help more families and businesses if they charged interest?

This is a powerful objection, but it is rooted in our flawed societal perspective. Some would argue that if we do not lend at interest to this family, then we may not be able to lend to the next family, and others will not lend freely either, therefore lending will cease altogether, and no one will be able to start a business or buy a home. This line of logic might be true (though the price of things would surely drop if this happened), yet it is only true because not enough people refuse to stop facilitating the system that has made homes and startup businesses so expensive in the first place.

Our Lord Jesus Christ calls us to be radically different from the world, for the world is the kingdom of the enemy. Usury, or lending at interest, is something that the world promotes and tells us we cannot live without. It is up to each of us to decide whether this is a lie from the enemy or just a fact of life. Would it be completely impossible for businesses to flourish and families to buy homes if modern-day lending ceased to exist? Or is it possible that we could all be a bit more charitable, and this charity would make things more obtainable for the masses?

I admit, getting the masses to adapt to these alternatives may be a pie-in-the-sky dream. This is why I focused on the stock market. It is much easier to personally divest than it is to detangle from the lending industry and from the entire finance industry, as my personal experience demonstrates. I included this chapter on usury to drive home the point that the financial practices we engage in are far from ideal.

I understand the points made by those who are convinced that lending at interest is necessary to modern-day society. I am sympathetic to those ideas. I am simply not convinced that modern-day financial practices are the best we can do for the common good, i.e., producing saints for the glory of God.

I am all for a lender giving to a borrower and reaping the reward of the borrower's success if the lender labors alongside the borrower in some capacity and assumes some risk. This is actually done in many lender-borrower relationships when the lender offers their expertise, guidance, and consulting to the borrower. The question is just how much is that money and expertise actually worth? In today's lending world, more often than not, the lender takes virtually no risk, no labor is done alongside the borrower, everything is based on greed instead of charity, and these conditions do not equate to good means and therefore, cannot justify good ends.

Good arguments for the acceptance of lending at interest can be found at Catholic.com (see specific links below), yet each of these writings condemn excessive rates of interest, whatever those may be.

- https://www.catholic.com/encyclopedia/interest-monetary
- https://www.catholic.com/magazine/print-edition/did-the-church-change-its-stance-on-usury
- https://www.catholic.com/magazine/print-edition/the-red-herring-of-usury

Fed Up On Usury,[14] published on NewPolity.com, offers an academic approach to the arguments I present in this book.

PARTING THOUGHTS

Why would any member of the Christian family deny that our economy ought to be based upon Matthew 5:42, where our Lord says, "Give to him who begs from you, and do not refuse him who would borrow from you"? A true Christian economy that works towards the common good is a gift economy that is based

14 Domencic, Sean. "Fed Up on Usury." Newpolity, https://newpolity.com/blog/fed-up-on-usury. Accessed November 12, 2023.

on the principal virtue of charity. Some may say a gift economy is financially imprudent, but true imprudence is to ignore our eternal future and the words of God. Shouldn't we live by example even if it costs us? Perhaps I am too zealous, but I have faith in our Lord when he claims that our Father in heaven will give us our daily bread, and I believe our Lord when he says, "Do not lay up for yourselves treasures on earth…lay up for yourselves treasures in heaven…For where your treasure is, there will your heart be also" (Mt 6:19-21).

The stock market and lending at interest use money to produce nothing but more money, and this contributes to inflation, cultivates vices, leads to abstract dominant economics, and assists in producing a globalized society. All of these things lead to family decay. As the family goes, so goes society. More importantly, though, as the family decomposes, so too does a reliable means for producing saints.

If my rationale for moral investing still has you in doubt, please honor this request: Consider spending a little time investigating the ideas I've put forth. Whether your reaction is indecisive or immediately resolute, I ask that you pray for an open heart and mind and seek counsel from other faithful Christians.

I am making this request knowing I can be impulsive and obsessive, attributes that have gotten me into trouble and led me to logical and theological errors. While I strive to become more patient and diligent, it is possible that I've overlooked points that could bolster my arguments. I trust that others making the case for moral investing will be compelling. Let's leave our biases at the door, discern the arguments to the best of our abilities, and ask for guidance from the Holy Spirit.

It is possible that even those with whom I agree may steer you and me wrong regarding stock market investing and usury.

Perhaps those who disagree with my arguments will steer you in the wrong direction, too. Heck, my arguments may be off kilter.

What we know for sure, however, is that our Lord will never steer us wrong. The truth will set us free, so go to Him: the Way, the Truth, and the Life!

ACKNOWLEDGEMENTS

I owe a great deal of gratitude to many people for making this book a reality. Chief among them is my wife, who supported and prayed for me every step of the way even when our family's financial situation was far less than comfortable. I would also like to thank newpolity.com for the great work they do, Bud MacFarlane and Xavier MacFarlane of the Mary Foundation for the countless hours spent preparing this work for publication, Matt and Emily D'Antuono for helping this book get off the ground, Lorraine Ranalli for her expert editing, and all the Christian thinkers who laid the groundwork for the ideas found in this book.

ABOUT THE AUTHOR

Marc Lozano is an atheist convert to Catholicism, who holds undergraduate and graduate degrees in business with focuses in finance. He had personal success playing the market and running a stock picking business called Christ Centered Capital that he later turned into a non-profit dedicated to the Christian view of wealth. He spent the early part of his career as a business operations manager for the National Basketball Association (NBA) until his efforts to disprove his wife's Catholic convictions led him back to the Church with fervor. He now manages business operations for several Catholic and non-denominational ministries. Marc lives in northeast Pennsylvania with his wife Taylor and their five children, Graciela, Magdalene, Rocco, Augustine, and Amora.